Latin American Fiction

Blackwell Introductions to Literature

This series sets out to provide concise and stimulating introductions to literary subjects. It offers books on major authors (from John Milton to James Joyce), as well as key periods and movements (from Old English literature to the contemporary). Coverage is also afforded to such specific topics as 'Arthurian Romance'. All are written by outstanding scholars as texts to inspire newcomers and others: non-specialists wishing to revisit a topic, or general readers. The overall aim is to ground and prepare students and readers of whatever kind in their pursuit of wider reading.

Published

Latin American Fiction

A Short Introduction

Philip Swanson

Blackwell Publishing

© 2005 by Philip Swanson

BLACKWELL PUBLISHING
350 Main Street, Malden, MA 02148-5020, USA
108 Cowley Road, Oxford OX4 1JF, UK
550 Swanston Street, Carlton, Victoria 3053, Australia

First published 2005 by Blackwell Publishing Ltd

Library of Congress Cataloging-in-Publication Data

Swanson, Philip, 1959–
  Latin American fiction : a short introduction / Philip Swanson.
      p. cm.—(Blackwell introductions to literature)
  Includes bibliographical references and index.
  ISBN 1-4051-0865-7 (hardback : alk. paper)—ISBN 1-4051-0866-5
(pbk. : alk. paper)   1. Spanish American fiction—20th century—History
and criticism.   2. Spanish American fiction—19th century—History
                and criticism. I. Title. II. Series.

PQ7082.N7S955   2004
863'.70998—dc22
2004011681

A catalogue record for this title is available from the British Library.

Set in 10/13pt Meridien
by Graphicraft Limited, Hong Kong
Printed and bound in the United Kingdom
by MPG Books, Bodmin, Cornwall

For further information on
Blackwell Publishing, visit our website:
www.blackwellpublishing.com

For Kaarina and Jo Jo

Contents

CHAPTER 1

Beginnings: Narrative and the Challenge of New Nations

The principal challenge of an introduction to Latin American fiction is to combine a clear and cohesive narrative history with a sensitivity towards the inevitably vast and varied nature of such a phenomenon. Take the very concept of 'Latin America' itself. The term refers to a huge subcontinent made up of many different regions and nations. Spanish is the principal language, but in the biggest country, Brazil, Portuguese is spoken. In the Caribbean meantime, other languages, such as French and English, are the national tongues of some states. Within many Spanish-speaking countries, especially Andean ones, various indigenous or 'Indian' languages are spoken. And when does 'Latin America' begin? Is one to include the period before the arrival of Columbus or can the word 'Latin' only refer to the post-Columbian experience? Are the writings of the colonial period Latin American or often merely Spanish (even if written in the so-called New World)? Do Latin American culture and identity really begin in the nineteenth century with Independence and/or with the forging of nation states? Is the term valid anyway or merely the projection of a colonial European mentality? Does it include or do justice to the ethnic range and mix of the subcontinent (for example, of indigenous, European, African, other or mixed descent)? And what about the increasingly Hispanicized USA? Is this also the locus of Latin American culture?

Unsurprisingly, the sorts of questions and issues raised here have led to long, fractious and often unresolved debates about the scope and nature of Latin American identity and culture. Indeed, with regard to literature, for instance, the last few decades of the twentieth century saw a growing trend in Latin American literary criticism away from synoptic histories or the discussion of broad movements towards instead highly contextualized studies of specific historical periods, genres and sub-genres, countries, areas (such as, say, Central America, the Caribbean, the Southern Cone) or social groupings. Still, despite its obvious shortcomings, the term 'Latin American fiction' is still widely used, even if it is often mainly applied to narratives written in Spanish from around Independence onwards. Moreover, contemporary critical accounts based on a discourse of marginality and exceptions, while often a valuable corrective, sometimes ignore the realities of literary history and the validity and importance of a coherent explanation of trends and patterns that do come to prominence and form part of what must ultimately be seen as a mainstream.

What follows here will, while retaining a consciousness of difference and the heterogeneous, generally seek to provide such an account of mainstream tendencies in Latin American fiction, concentrating (largely, though not exclusively) on writing in Spanish from the nineteenth century onwards.[1] That account is based on an acceptance that the rise of the Latin American New Novel and the Boom of the 1960s (which brought to international attention writers such as Gabriel García Márquez and Mario Vargas Llosa) represent, in literary-historical terms, the most significant developments ever in Latin American writing. However, the New Novel did not grow out of or remain in a historical vacuum (literary or political). The character of Latin American narrative was in many ways shaped by the experiences of colonialism and independence, the relationship – perceived as both positive and negative – with Europe, and the tensions surrounding modernization and the consolidation of national identities. Thus the evolution of Latin American fiction will be examined first in the context of developments in the nineteenth and early twentieth centuries. It will also be considered in terms of what happened after the Boom, a period of both refinement of and reaction against the New Novel. Moreover, the discussion will be extended to include Hispanic fiction from the US. Finally, given the obvious potentially polemical nature of any discussion of fiction from Latin America, we will also examine briefly the ways in which 'Latin American fiction' functions as a concept in society, the market and the academy, and address the very legitimacy of a project that seeks to offer an expository survey of the nature of Latin American fiction.

The Nineteenth Century

The history of Latin American fiction has to be understood in two broad and interrelated contexts: the socio-political and the literary. This seemingly straightforward contention is far from uncontroversial in the Latin American context. A common argument to explain the success of thé New Novel and the Boom is that such fiction constituted a rejection of a previous tradition of instructional narrative, designed to teach patriotic lessons or offer ideological challenges to them, in favour of a more fundamentally literary approach in which language and fiction were playfully or experimentally liberated from a narrow and local social context. This in turn led to a backlash after the Boom, with such a position being attacked as elitist, Eurocentric and in denial of cultural specificity. Needless to say, there is something of truth in both perspectives. Many developments in Latin American writing are a function of an essentially *literary* history, but it is undeniable and crucial to realize that literary history in the region is often inextricably bound up with issues of society and politics. In the colonial period, for example, the first books were largely designed to aid in the evangelization of the natives, and the diaries, chronicles and other narratives of the era were often basically an expression of the mentality of the occupying colonizers. But even at this early stage there were tensions. The most renowned document of this period is probably *El lazarillo de los ciegos caminantes* (tr. 'A Guide for Inexperienced Travellers Between Buenos Aires and Lima', 1775 or 1776) by Concolocorvo (real name Alonso Carrió de la Vandera, c.1715–c.1778). This travel narrative with novelistic flourishes echoes the Spanish picaresque tradition and also functions as an official report for the viceregal authorities. However, it is also highly satirical and gestures towards the ignorance of the colonizers and the honourable nature of local practices and values. None the less, it is not until the nineteenth century that a more obviously political literature begins to emerge in tandem with a republican spirit seeking to foster a new sense of nationhood.

Civilization and Barbarism

In conceptual terms, the cornerstone text of Latin American fiction (as well as of other areas of literature, arts and thought) is undoubtedly

Facundo, produced in 1845 by the Argentine Domingo Faustino Sarmiento (1811–88). Sarmiento's book is not really a novel as such but a peculiar hybrid of fiction, history and essay, and its importance lies in its ideological content rather than its intrinsically literary qualities. It is a work born of political circumstances and historical change, specifically the opportunities, challenges, threats and anxieties surrounding Independence. The Wars of Independence in the early nineteenth century (more or less between 1810 and 1825, with Independence completed in most places by 1828)[2] marked a desire for freedom from colonial restraint and the authority of the Spanish crown. However, the wars were essentially promoted and prosecuted by the white *criollo* or creole elites of European descent, who essentially sought to secure the control of trade, wealth and power for an American-born ruling class.

'Independence' was thus a problematic concept. Despite the discourse of liberty and (often quite genuine) political idealism, independence was, in practice, more immediately significant for the few rather than the many and had little real meaning for the ordinary, indigenous or mixed-race masses, who, even after Independence, continued to suffer under a system of extreme social hierarchy, a semi-feudal agricultural sector, racial division and, in some areas, even slavery. The result was that Independence often brought with it unrest and instability, and the key concern for so-called liberal thinkers in the period after it was how to achieve stability, progress and modernization on, say, a British, French or North American model in newly emerging nations characterized by difference and strife. The growth of a print press had already helped fuel republican discourse and the beginnings of a new sense of national identification, but now, increasingly, literary or semi-literary texts were produced to foster national identities and the sort of national values the educated writing and reading classes wished to project for the new prototype nations with which they were associated. In other words, 'literature', for want of a better term, became a major force in nation-building or the forging of what Benedict Anderson has famously termed 'imagined communities' – a now much-touted notion in Latin American cultural criticism referring to the kind of ideal or aspirational national social order that writers and intellectuals hoped or wished to come into being.

The background to *Facundo* is post-Independence Argentina. The region now called Argentina was torn by quarrels in this period between liberals and conservatives, leading to a series of wars between

1820 and 1870 involving two main sides, known as Unitarians and Federalists. The first group were largely city-based liberal intellectuals who supported the idea of a centralized state run from the capital Buenos Aires, while the second were often rural landowners who preferred a decentralized system of more or less autonomous provinces which would safeguard their own local power. The clash between the two groups was often presented as one between pro-European modernization and progress on the one hand, and xenophobic Catholic traditionalism on the other – a clash in other words between the forces of what could be termed 'civilization' and 'barbarism'. Indeed this conflict gave the name to the subtitle of Sarmiento's seminal work: *Facundo o civilización y barbarie* ('Facundo, or Civilization and Barbarism'). From now on, 'Civilization and Barbarism' would become a stock phrase in and theme of Latin American writing and thought. It expressed, in the initial stages of the term's development, a concern about the future direction of newly emancipated Latin American nations, as the elite attempted to build on a rather precarious sense of order and 'civilization' (associated with the 'progressive' urban metropolis) which was thought to be under threat from the disorderly example of the wild, untamed, 'barbaric' – and often native or part-native – masses (associated with the undeveloped interior).[3]

The embodiment of 'barbarism' in the Argentine context was a provinicial caudillo or boss figure called Juan Manuel de Rosas, who eventually became a ruling dictator (in differing contexts from 1829 to 1833 and from 1833 to 1852). Rosas built on his early power base of rural gauchos to develop a huge mass movement, structured around a hysterical personality cult and supported by fanaticism, terror and the forced expulsion of his opponents. Though Rosas eventually fell from power and though Sarmiento himself later became president of a now united republic, the cult of the dictator is seen by many as casting a long shadow over Argentine history and contributing to a cultural pattern that would later lead, in the twentieth century, to phenomena such as Peronism, military dictatorship and the Falklands/Malvinas debacle. Indeed this cultural pattern soon came to be linked by writers and thinkers with the Latin American subcontinent as a whole. Not surprisingly, then, the theme of Civilization and Barbarism influenced thought and literature well beyond the mid-nineteenth century Southern Cone and – in various forms and with various revisions and permutations – would become one of the main prisms

through which Latin American literature and culture came to be ana-
lysed and understood.

Sarmiento's book actually focuses on one of Rosas' rivals (and,
ultimately, victims), Facundo Quiroga, another country landlord and
gaucho leader. It sets Facundo's rise to power against the often gory
background of life on the Argentine *pampa* or grasslands, but also
charts his downfall at the hands of Rosas. By the end Rosas has
become a dangerous national incarnation of Facundo's barbarism,
while the liberal alternative of the likes of Sarmiento is projected as
the only antidote to his institutionalized destructiveness and cruelty.
This alternative is symbolized by Buenos Aires itself, presented as the
opposite of rural barbarism, a thriving capital and port characterized
by budding modernity, new thinking and a trading culture which also
implies a transatlantic awareness and openness to European and North
American values.[4] It is easy to see how *Facundo* came to be seen as
the fullest expression of the idea that the only way forward for the
newly independent nations of Latin America was the advancement of
(usually) coastal city-based, European-influenced, economic, political,
social, intellectual and moral values, via the taming of the terrifying
propensity for the undisciplined barbarism of the native or near-
native interior that constantly threatened to unseat a newly created
and highly vulnerable system of civilized society.

This reading of Sarmiento was to have enormous impact. A wealth
of fiction would revisit the civilization-versus-barbarism theme in both
the nineteenth and twentieth centuries, and in some ways this theme
would be the dominant one of the Latin American 'classics' of the
first half of the twentieth century. But literary and other writings
would also challenge this version of Sarmiento, in particular the perception that the humble gaucho was the source of the nation's ills.
Not only did this lead to much revisionist 'gauchesque' literature in
Argentina (most notably the great book-length epic poem *El gaucho
Martín Fierro* ['The Gaucho Martín Fierro', 1872 and 1879] by José
Hernández [1834–86]), in which central government was portrayed
as itself the bringer of social unrest by its annihilation of traditional
national cultures; it also laid the ground for an entire way of debating
the very nature of Latin American culture and identity that is still
very much alive right up to the present day. The irony is that the
negative reading of Sarmiento's position is something of a caricature
and his stance is often quite ambiguous. In many ways, Sarmiento's

notion of barbarism was simply the abandonment of responsible government as personified in Rosas. And though he did himself caricature the gauchos, *Facundo*, especially in its early stages, often seems to romanticize the longstanding gaucho way of life. It may even appear to mythicize the caudillo figure via the exaggeration of the cult of Quiroga. The point is that Sarmiento was, as a literary writer, a man of his times. Romanticism (especially French Romanticism in the Southern Cone) was an important cultural influence in Latin America from the 1830s onwards and writers like Sarmiento, despite hard-nosed political concerns, were unable to avoid some degree of romanticization of the past as well as the visionary future.

Spanish America's first major Romantic writer was Esteban Echeverría (1805–51). However, he is probably best remembered for a short narrative that predates *Facundo* and offers a more accessible if cruder anticipation of Sarmiento's Civilization and Barbarism ethic, *El matadero* (1838). The title refers to a slaughterhouse and this stands as an allegory of the nation under Rosas. The *'pequeña república'* or mini-republic of the abattoir is run by an all-powerful master-butcher who oversees an assortment of grotesque butchers in typical provincial garb and vile, filthy labourers scrapping over animal waste – an unmistakable echo of Rosas, caudillos and their gaucho followers: 'simulacro en pequeño era éste del modo bárbaro con que se ventilan en nuestro país las cuestiones y los derechos individuales y sociales' ('this was a microcosm of the barbaric manner in which matters concerning individual and social issues and rights are aired in our country').[5] The brain-washing mystique of Rosas is reflected in the portrayal of the ordinary folk as equivalent to cattle who passively go to their slaughter. One bull, described as being as stubborn as a Unitarian, stands out and refuses to give in, but its eventual capture and castration clearly represent the emasculation of decent liberal values.

A similar fate befalls a real-life Unitarian in the tale. In contrast to the mindless slogan-chanting and sporting of pro-Rosas emblems of the butchering masses, the Unitarian is civilized, well-spoken and elegantly dressed. Like the virile and independent-minded bull, this man has 'cojones' or balls and is willing to stand out from the conformist crowd. He finally dies following a fit of rage, when his savage torturers perform a metaphorical castration by stripping him and cutting off the whiskers he wears in the Unitarian style. None the less, and foreshadowing the epilogue of *Facundo*, this fine man is compared in his torment by the mob to Jesus on the cross (p. 159), underscoring the importance of the class he represents as not only the unfair victim but also the potential saviour of the nation. Echeverría's tone is more consistently extreme than that of Sarmiento, but in a sense his real message is the same: his *Dogma socialista* (1837) reveals a notion of 'sociability' (rather than socialism in the modern sense) which posits the ideal of a mutually respectful society based on fairness and social cohesion.[6]

The ideas of Echeverría and the more influential Sarmiento are conceptually foundational to the development of fiction in Latin America. However, the first real Latin American novel predates them and predates Independence. It is *El periquillo sarniento* ('The Itching Parrot', 1816) by the Mexican José Joaquín Fernández de Lizardi (1776–1827).[7] Though the novel is little studied and was probably of little real impact, it is an interesting forerunner of the concerns about nation that would come to characterize later novels of the nineteenth century and beyond. Having said that, it is really rooted – echoing Concolocorvo – in the Spanish tradition of picaresque novels such as *Lazarillo de Tormes* (1554). Like Lazarillo, Lizardi's protagonist Periquillo follows a series of jobs (for example, student, monk, judge, soldier, pharmacist, doctor's assistant, tradesman, barber, beggar and crook) in a largely episodic narrative that allows for a wide range of social satirical observations bringing out the hypocrisy of Mexican society. The social satire, though, albeit derivative in a literary sense, actually gives the novel a degree of national focus. Periquillo's range of adventures can be seen as an embryonic tracing of an imagined emerging nation and as a commentary on the type of society that is emerging. There is virtually no explicit excitement about the idea of Independence here, but the satire surrounding the 'hero''s apprenticeship in life does encapsulate *criollo* concerns about the barrier to their own social and economic progress represented by the colonial system, as well as offering a morally corrective perspective on the *criollo* class. From this point of view, *El periquillo sarniento* can be seen as anticipating or even paving the way for subsequent narrative of a more explicitly nationalist persuasion.[8]

National romances

As has already been hinted with regard to Echeverría and Sarmiento, 'nationalist' writing was very much bound up with Romanticism.

Romanticism was always wrapped up in concerns about changing values after the Enlightenment and the aftermath of the French Revolution in Europe, leading to either a sense of malaise or idealism. In Latin America these mixed feelings were projected, especially by liberal intellectuals with a vocation of civic obligation, on to the new nations, with the result that those narratives which could – to a greater or lesser extent – be described as Romantic tended to offer an idealistic map for national evolution coupled with an anxiety about its possible failure. The differing portrayal of the gaucho – barbaric threat or romantic repository of national tradition – is a case in point.[9]

In Brazil, the figure of the Indian offered the potential for similar ambiguities. In reality, Indianist literature or *indianismo* was largely escapist and with little social content, its sources being Longfellow, Fenimore Cooper and Chateaubriand as much as Brazilian society. None the less, Indians did become a projected emblem of national identity, largely because – unlike the non-native black slaves from Africa – they could be taken as authentically Brazilian while remaining conveniently distant and exotic. In *O Guaraní* (1857), José Martiniano de Alencar (1829–77), Brazil's major Romantic novelist, envisions a kind of ideal world of harmony between Indians and Portuguese, but his best-known work, *Iracema* (1865), is more uncertain. Here an Indian princess, Iracema, falls in love with a white man, Martim, but as a result is forced to abandon her community. The couple have a son, Moacir, who might be seen as emblematic of a positive future for an authentic mixed-race nation. However, such optimism may be neutralized by the fact that Iracema dies as a result of the birth. She is effectively assimilated and then killed off. Her fate surely calls into question the meaningfulness or even possibility of any potential ideal transcultural state.

This intriguing mixture of ill-fated love story and ambivalent national allegory was pretty typical of a number of Spanish American novels of the same period, most notably the two great national romances *Amalia* (1851), by Argentina's José Mármol (1818–71), and *María* (1867), by Colombia's Jorge Isaacs (1837–95). In an important revisionist study of the genre, *Foundational Fictions*, Doris Sommer contends that the mid-century fashion for novels about young lovers wooing each other across class, regional or racial divides was a projection of a desire for nation-building and national conciliation. The romantic love theme is really about, then, the need to court and

domesticate civil society after the *criollo*s had won independence
(Sommer 1991, p. 6).[10]

The earlier novel, *Amalia*, has a much more obvious political focus.
Set against the background of the Rosas dictatorship, it deals with an
abortive Unitarian conspiracy against the dictator in 1840. In many
ways, it is a historical novel with much overwhelming detail of life
in Buenos Aires under the dictatorship and a wealth of historical
characters, including Rosas himself and his deliciously wicked sister-
in-law María Josefa Ezcurra. The political dimension of the plot
centres on one Daniel Bello's scheming against the system. But if
Daniel is heroic, he does not really achieve very much. Moreover,
the Unitarian perspective of the novel risks creating an impression of
neo-aristocratic moral superiority (particularly with regard to race).
Equally awkward is the weaving into this historical framework of the
love story involving Daniel's allies, Eduardo Belgrano and Amalia.
Even so, the love plot can be read politically. Eduardo is a wounded
plotter who is cared for by the eponymous Amalia, but ultimately
forced into exile: the lovers' curtailed domestic idyll may therefore be
a manifestation of the positive national values associated with the
Unitarian cause that are threatened by the savagery of the regime.
Significantly too, Amalia is from the interior while Eduardo is from
the capital. Their romance is thus an expression of the desire for an
ideal state of the nation in which the conflict between 'civilization'
and 'barbarism' is resolved. But, of course, Amalia is no barbarian and
certainly no gaucho: the national conciliation sought is really more
the wished-for triumph of the values of the pro-European elite.

In *María* the love story is much more to the fore, and in this sense
this is probably a more successfully worked and less diffuse novel –
even though its narrative structure is rather loose, with its meander-
ing, descriptive passages and sub-plots. It was (and, to some extent,
remains) hugely popular and is widely regarded as Latin America's
great Romantic novel. At the same time, this makes it a rather
unlikely candidate for a nation-building narrative. For a start, it may
be seen as just a love story. It is about the love of a young man,
Efraín, for the orphan girl, María, whom his father has taken in as
his ward. Despite the fact that they are like brother and sister, the
parents agree to their wish to marry as long as Efraín first finishes his
education in London so as subsequently to establish himself back
home. Unfortunately, María has a hereditary disease of sorts (in fact,

epilepsy) and – tragically – dies before Efraín returns. This inexplicable tragic ending also dilutes the national dimension in that it seems to present the star-crossed lovers as victims of an arbitrary curse of destiny rather than of social circumstances – something underlined by the symbolism of the 'ave negra' or black bird which appears menacingly as an image of a dark fate at key moments of misfortune in the novel. The setting of *María*, nevertheless, on a slave plantation, should alert us to a possibly significant social, economic and political context, and Sommer, indeed, offers a persuasive political reading of the novel. The very fact that the lovers' idyll takes place on a near-feudal slave plantation and that there are precious few references to Colombia's political and economic difficulties suggest that *María*'s largely first-person narrative is characterized by a nostalgic or anxious harking back to the colonial heritage of slave owning, before abolition initiated a radical transformation in class culture. It is a novel, in other words, of the fears and anxieties about the building of a new nation based on racial mix. The inherited disease is a metaphorical symptom of the withering of what was essentially an aristocracy.

Another novel worthy of consideration in the context of Romantic fiction and narratives of slavery is *Sab*, published rather earlier than *Amalia* or *María*, in 1841, by the Cuban Gertrudis Gómez de Avellaneda (1814–73). Avellaneda actually spent most of her adult life in Spain and it is not clear that *Sab* was especially influential in the development of Latin American fiction, but it has received considerable critical attention and been consequently canonized from the late twentieth century onwards, following the rise in academic literary critical circles of feminism and postcolonialism.[11] The novel is usually read as an abolitionist anti-slavery work that draws a parallel between the position of the slave in Cuba and woman in a patriarchal society. Indeed the comparison is explicit: 'como los esclavos ellas [las mujeres] arrastran pacientemente su cadena y bajan la cabeza bajo el yugo de las leyes humanas' ('just like the slaves, they [women] patiently drag along their chains and bow their head beneath the yoke of the laws of men') (p. 194). The apparent emphasis on slavery and the position of women explains much of the novel's contemporary appeal to critics, but equally appealing to them is the opportunity offered by the text for historical revisionism. Like *Amalia*, the historical setting is quite explicit for a novel often Romantic in character. The main action is on a slave plantation in Cuba in the early nineteenth century when the island was still a Spanish colony. It concerns a mulatto slave, Sab, and his impossible love for his master's white daughter Carlota. Carlota agrees to marry the grasping materialist Englishman Enrique Otway. The marriage is jeopardized when Enrique discovers that Carlota is not as rich as he thought, but is finally made possible after Sab secretly donates his winning national lottery ticket to Carlota. In true Romantic style, Sab dies the very moment that the couple wed.

What is interesting about this story is that it actually sets events in a much wider context than slavery alone. This is really another book about the decline of the landowning classes as they become vulnerable to economic modernization and the demands of foreign commercial interests. In allegorical terms, the beautiful *criolla*[12] Carlota is the prize of Cuba, built up with the support of a slave economy, and now open to exploitation by mercenary foreign entrepreneurs (Enrique). The 'Carta de Sab a Teresa' ('Letter from Sab to Teresa [Carlota's cousin]') which concludes the novel may well be an echo of the Latin American Independence hero Simón Bolívar's famous *Carta de Jamaica* ('Letter from Jamaica') of 1815, in which he outlined his core political beliefs (Hart 1999, p. 72), and therefore a veiled gesture (Avellaneda was, remember, based in Spain) towards the cause of Independence. Sab himself gains independence in the novel when he is freed. But it is at the level of race and slavery that the novel's main ambiguities can be seen. Sab is a rather unlikely character. Intelligent and honourable, he is really a projection of Rousseau's noble savage (a figure so dear to the Romantics) – a fantasy of liberal white desire for reform without loss of privilege. Indeed his behaviour is almost that of the ideal white man and it should come as no surprise that he is particularly light-skinned. The other slaves, meanwhile, are often portrayed as passive and essentially contented. And Sab, is, in any case, just like any other Romantic hero – ultimately a victim of love and fate (hence his melodramatic death) as much as of society.

Despite any such revisionist reservations about the limitations of Avellaneda's social perspective, there can be no doubt that *Sab* remains a striking example of the literature of national reflection, not least because of the centrality of a black character at the heart of the narrative and its unquestionable abolitionist thrust. The fact is, though, that in its day it was very much the work of a Cuban in Spain. It did not have a great degree of impact in the years after her death, though slavery was at last abolished in Cuba some thirteen years later in 1886.

Costumbrismo

What is true of *Sab*, and of all the major texts considered here so far, is that, despite varying degrees of connection to the idea of Romanticism, they are all very much concerned (even *María*) with the social, economic, political and geographical reality of Latin America. Indeed, later, more experimental literary reactions against first nineteenth-century and thereafter early twentieth-century writing have tended to be explained in terms of a rejection of the instructional, patriotic, national or, broadly speaking, 'realistic' nature of such writing. Given that post-Independence nineteenth-century narrative of note was always, to a greater or lesser extent, bound up with the legitimization of new nations or the expression of aspirational ideals for them, it is not surprising that it also seeks to be something of a reflection of reality. For example, much nineteenth-century narrative was heavily influenced by *costumbrismo* or costumbrism. *Costumbrismo* was a type of literature that paid particular attention to the customs or habits of a particular region or, later, country, and is often associated with the depiction of picturesque scenes of local colour. In Spain, for example, portraits of rural Andalucía, such as *Cuadros de costumbres* ('Sketches of Customs and Manners', published in 1857, though written earlier) by Fernán Caballero (the pen name of Cecilia Francisca Boehl von Faber [1796–1877]), had significant impact (Caballero was a friend of Gómez de Avellaneda), as did the more analytical sketches of Mariano José de Larra (1809–37).

'New World' writers soon followed the Spanish example as costumbrism was applied to the demand after Independence for vivid portraits of a specifically Latin American reality. In fact, all of the works discussed so far contain obviously costumbrist elements, with their eloquent descriptions of, say, gaucho life on the *pampa* or plantation society.[13] But perhaps the most quintessential Latin American manifestation of *costumbrismo* was the *tradición* (traditional sketch), associated nowadays almost exclusively with the Peruvian Ricardo Palma (1833–1919). His *Tradiciones peruanas* ('Traditional Sketches of Peru', published over a lengthy period between 1872 and 1910) were colourful and witty pieces which focused on the historical past, usually the colonial period, though sometimes the pre-Columbian or post-Independence eras. They covered the whole range of Peruvian society from vagabond to viceroy, were often of a satirical bent, and dealt with a variety of anecdotes concerning social disagreements, religious practices, popular linguistic expressions and the like. In effect, what they did was to supply the padding of a national tradition for the new Peruvian nation and help in the forging of a sense of national identity. But also, in expanding the scope of *costumbrismo* (which tended towards the escapist), they provided a bridge between Romanticism and Realism, as a more recognizably realist style of literature began to come to dominance (with some, as shall later be seen, major exceptions) in the late nineteenth and early twentieth centuries.

Realist narratives

Talking about Latin American realist fiction is really rather problematic. As has been indicated, many later writers would regard the works considered so far as very much connected to social reality, while many of the major so-called realist novels to appear in Latin America after Romanticism do not really stand comparison with the European Realism of, say, Balzac, Dickens or Galdós, or the Naturalism of, say, Zola or the early Pardo Bazán. A looser, broader and less historically specific notion of realism (with a small r) may well be a more helpful way of understanding the evolution of Latin American fiction from the late nineteenth to the mid twentieth centuries. In the meantime, though, three transitional figures should be briefly mentioned.

The Chilean Alberto Blest Gana (1829–1904) is usually credited with producing the first European-style Realist novel in the form of *Martín Rivas* (1862). Romance and sentiment are not entirely absent from this novel, but it echoes very much Dickensian Realism, with its eponymous hero pursuing a trajectory from the shabbier and semi-dependent end of society to the point of entry into mainstream upper middle-class society, against a background of colourful lower-class rogues and saucier sorts providing lighter relief. The main Naturalist writer of the period is probably Argentina's Eugenio Cambaceres (1843–89). His *Sin Rumbo* ('Without Direction', 1885) is a dark novel dwelling, in a kind of perverse realignment of the *costumbrista* tradition, on the sordid and often unspeakably violent detail of human reality, while his *En la sangre* ('In the Blood', 1887) clearly alludes to that other Naturalist credo of hereditary determinism. The last notable Naturalist novel was probably the Mexican Federico Gamboa's (1864–1939) *Santa* (1903). However, despite its emphasis on the squalid and deterministic, Shaw sees it as marking a kind of swansong for

Naturalism because of its tendency towards the love ideal and moral regeneration (Shaw 2002, pp. 30–2).

The problem is that none of the preceding titles can be seen as great novels and they have received scant critical attention so far. They did form part of a strand of development in Latin American fiction that continued into the twentieth century (the grotesque realism of the later Boom writer José Donoso's first novel, *Coronación* ['Coronation', 1957], being a striking case in point), but never helped create a really strong trend for urban or provincial Realism or Naturalism in the European tradition. What the brief burgeoning of Realism and Naturalism at the turn of the century did show, however, was that a concern with social reality was becoming a self-consciously central feature of Latin American fiction.

Perhaps a more interesting example of fiction of a sort of Realist-Naturalist inclination, and perhaps more typical of the kind of direction Latin American realism would broadly take after the nineteenth century, was Clorinda Matto de Turner's (Peru, 1852–1909) *Aves sin nido* ('Birds without a Nest', 1889). Although its feet are still partly in the costumbrist and even Romantic camps, *Aves sin nido* sees itself as a departure from the norm. In her preface to the novel, Matto emphasizes two things. One is what might be called realism: to describe her literary aims she uses words like 'fotografía' ('photograph'), 'observar atentamente' ('careful observation'), 'exactitud' ('exactness') and 'copia' ('copy'). The other is social protest: she expresses her love of the indigenous people and her hatred of tyranny (which she associates with the church, government and landowners), and wishes her work to offer a 'moraleja correctiva' ('moral corrective') that will help to 'mejorar la condición de los pueblos chicos del Perú' ('improve the condition of the communities of the Peruvian interior') and contribute to 'los progresos nacionales' ('national progress').[14] The text that follows her introductory remarks may not fit the classic critical definition, but what emerges here is a consciousness of a kind of social realism that is not only a first step in the development of Indigenism but was to become, in general terms, characteristic of much Latin American fiction for the next half century or so. Unlike the romantic projections of Brazilian *indianismo, indigenismo* sought to combine a more realistic presentation of the 'Indian'[15] experience with social and political critique. Indigenism became a genuine phenomenon in the first half of the twentieth century, but Matto's work clearly anticipates it.

It has become fashionable to point out the limitations of Indigenist writing, emphasizing the sometime tendency to idealize the Indians and the paternalistic or maternalistic outside perspective of writers who were usually white, urban and middle-class. Both things are true of *Aves sin nido*, and its explicit political preaching further limits its status as major literature. But for its time, it is a fierce and powerful piece of work (Matto was excommunicated and exiled for her troubles). In a sense the novel revisits the theme of Civilization and Barbarism, this time in an Andean context and with a tweaking of Sarmiento's perspective. There is a clear progressive, modernizing agenda here, but the presumptuous nature of a concept like civilization is implied, while, more importantly, barbarism, or *salvajismo* (wildness or possibly savagery) as Matto prefers to call it, is not inherent in rural folk but precisely a result of and reflection of their appalling mistreatment by the authorities. The barbaric exploitation of the Indians is the key background to the plot of the narrative. Lucía Marín is a white woman who temporarily relocates to the fictional Andean village of Kíllac because of her husband's mining interests. Her attempt to help the local Indian Yupanqui family results in a violent backlash in which the Yupanquis are killed and the Marín home is attacked. Lucía adopts the Yupanquis' daughters and takes them away from the mountains to the city – away from barbarism to a (hopefully) more enlightened, liberal urban culture.

The gendered perspective of the novel (with the positive emphasis on Lucía and other female characters) can also be taken as a wider expression of the hope for change and progress. But the ending introduces another negative. The birds without a nest of the title are obviously the orphaned Yupanqui girls. However, at the end the image undergoes an adjustment. Young Margarita Yupanqui is to marry the (also adopted) modern lawyer Manuel, but it is dramatically revealed that both are in fact the offspring of Kíllac's corrupt bishop. The young lovers are now referred to as the 'aves sin nido' of the title (p. 220). Once again the threat of incest is raised as a barrier to human happiness (as in *María* or even *Sab*, where Sab and Carlota are possibly cousins). But the incest theme here seems emptied of any Romantic overtones of cursed destiny. Here instead it is a searing reminder of very earthly injustices – the corruption of the church, the brutal attitude to women, and more generally the very lack of civility in the new nations that is such a threat to progress.

Matto's brand of realism may be too didactic or melodramatic for some tastes, while that of Blest Gana and Cambaceres may be too derivative or, even, uninteresting. However, there is one stand-alone figure in Latin American nineteenth-century Realism who could, without exaggeration, be easily mentioned in the same breath as Flaubert, and that is the Brazilian Joaquim Maria Machado de Assis (1839–1908). His mature works are not only masterpieces of Realism but also go much further, anticipating the profoundly modern style of literature that would characterize the most internationally famous Latin American novels of the twentieth century. His greatest work is *Dom Casmurro* (1899). At first sight it is typical of the sort of female-adultery novels that were successful in nineteenth-century Europe, such as Flaubert's *Madame Bovary* (1856) and the Portuguese Eça de Queiroz's (1845–1900) *O primo Basílio* ('Cousin Basílio', 1878). The solitary and ageing first-person narrator, Bento Santiago, the Dom Casmurro of the title, tells the story of his love for his childhood playmate Capitu. This seems like an echo of many other nineteenth-century novels, but there is a twist: Bento's account shows how, after marrying him, Capitu betrayed him by having an affair with his best friend Escobar.

The real twist, though, is embedded in the narrative perspective itself: the alert reader will see through Bento's version of events and conclude that his description of Capitu is a distortion of the facts, the manifestation of a manipulative and paranoically jealous mind. The reader needs to read between the lines. For example, if Bento's suspicions are examined closely it can be seen that they are initially aroused by nothing more than a look in Capitu's eyes; and when he suspects that his son Ezequiel is really a bastard because of a resemblance to Escobar, the reader ought to remember the narrative's numerous references to unexpected physical likenesses and the fact that such likenesses exist only in the eye of the beholder (let alone Escobar's suggestion that their children should intermarry, most unlikely if he were Ezequiel's real father). There are, in fact, many hints at Bento's immaturity and childish imagination. Moreover, it becomes apparent that, in writing in the present about the past, he is projecting on to the story of Capitu present feelings which may not even have existed at the time. On the final page of the novel, Bento addresses the reader directly: 'tu concordarás comigo: se te lembras bem da Capitu menina, hás de reconhecer que uma estava dentro da outra, como a fruta dentro da casca' ('you will agree with me: if you remember Capitu the girl, you must perforce recognize that the one was already inside the other, just as a piece of fruit is always already inside its husk').[16] Bento here clearly foreshadows the unreliable narrator of modern narrative, persuading the reader to accept a dubious and doctored interpretation of reality as truth. In this sense, Machado is stretching the boundaries of conventional realism and enticing the reader into a world of ambiguities and multiple points of view that would later become the main feature of the New Narrative of the mid-twentieth century.

Having said the above, this does not mean that *Dom Casmurro* is an utter problematization of the realist project. As with other stories of domestic love considered here, the novel has a very definite social, economic, political and historical context. It is set during the *Segundo Reinado* or Second Reign (1840–89), when Brazil was an empire, a kind of constitutional monarchy headed by Pedro II – a system that was more representative in theory than in practice. The economy during this period was dependent on slave labour and the export of sugar and coffee. The eventual abolition of slavery in 1888 is generally seen as hastening the collapse of the empire and the creation of a republic in 1889. Although Machado's novel is set in Rio de Janeiro, Bento's wealth is based on inheritance from a *fazenda* or plantation economy. The novel's background detail and the implied decadence of Bento may encourage us to read it as a commentary on the decline of the oligarchy and the empire it supported, as the slave-driven *fazenda* economy wanes and a new mercantile economy emerges. The patriarchal family with which Bento is associated is thus an allegory for an entire system struggling with a painful process of erosion and change. Such an allegorical reading might not be entirely surprising if one considers what is known about the life of Machado de Assis himself. Machado was a mulatto (and a dreadfully short-sighted epileptic with a stutter to boot) who, none the less, discreetly made his way up the Brazilian social ladder to become a significant player in white society. *Dom Casmurro* may well be – though this is speculation – a sly or nervous comment on the culture of dissimulation in later nineteenth-century Brazil and on the treacherously shifting sands of politics and economics on which that culture was precariously built.

One important thing to note about the two re-readings of *Dom Casmurro* mentioned here is that virtually nobody seemed to notice the possibility of them until the later twentieth century. Helen

Caldwell's *The Brazilian Othello of Machado de Assis*, published in the USA in 1960, was the first work to reveal the implied second narrative of *Dom Casmurro* in which an insanely jealous husband seeks to frame his innocent wife. And John Gledson's *The Deceptive Realism of Machado de Assis*, published in the UK in 1984, was the first – albeit building on Brazilian critic Roberto Schwarz's work on Machado's earlier fiction – to uncover the historical-political dimension.[17] This raises interesting questions about the nature of literary criticism as applied to Latin America (of which more in chapter 7), but may also explain why Machado is less well-known than he perhaps deserves. Not only was he writing in Portuguese, and moreover in Brazil, but also his work was probably taken largely at face value by his contemporaries. It is possibly for this reason that Machado was not the huge influence on the development of modern writing that he might otherwise have been. It was not until the Boom of the 1960s that Latin American fiction came to be widely associated with modernist experimental-ism, and it was only in the 1940s and 1950s that greatly influential evidence of experimental fiction can be plainly identified on any scale. For the time being, at the end of the nineteenth century and well into the first half of the twentieth century, the realist thrust remained the dominant strain in Latin American letters.

This last assertion might seem surprising to some scholars of Latin American literature. The reason for such surprise would be the curious emergence at the turn of the century of what was known as *modernismo*, followed by the rise of the so-called *vanguardia* or Latin American avant-garde in the early twentieth century. Recent criticism has, rightly, seen these movements not as the self-contained phenomena they have sometimes been thought to be, but as the first signs of a genuinely modernist aesthetic in Latin American literary production. However, the strength of *modernismo* and the *vanguardia* lies mainly in their poetry: the *modernista* and avant-garde novel – despite recent attempts at critical re-evaluation – represents more of a subterranean tendency. These movements will therefore be considered later, when focusing more acutely on the rise of modern fiction in Latin America in reaction against the perceived dominance of realism (chapter 3). The reality is that, as the first decades of the twentieth century unfolded, the main emphasis of canonical Latin American fiction continued to be the exploration of emerging national identities within the framework of an attempted realist model.

CHAPTER 2

National Narratives: Regional and Continental Identities

For literary critics, the dawn of the twentieth century in Latin America is usually marked by the turn-of-the-century movement of *modernismo*. This was traditionally seen as a self-contained phenomenon running, roughly, from the 1880s to around the time of World War I. It was conventionally thought to be characterized by a purely 'art for art's sake' aesthetic as a reaction against the national and instructional nature of what was perceived as the official or classical Latin American literature of the nineteenth century. A different but related phenomenon would be the advent of the *vanguardia* or Latin American avant-garde (with which Brazilian *modernismo*, starting in the 1920s, can also be identified). This broad movement or, rather, trend was usually seen as characterized by the adoption of the aesthetic of the European avant-garde, with its emphasis on stylistic innovation and radical break with tradition. Both these tendencies will be considered in more detail in the next chapter, as they can be seen as part of a literary genealogy leading to the eventual rise of the experimental New Narrative in Latin America in the 1940s and 1950s, culminating in the Boom of the 1960s. Though both trends did produce novels, their main output was actually poetry – so much so that one leading critic, for example, has stated that the vanguard novel only really existed between parentheses.[1]

The point is that the nation-building narratives of the nineteenth century led to an essentially realist tradition in which the most important fiction of the early twentieth century continued to dwell on questions of national identity as yet unresolved in the rapidly changing and modernizing countries of Latin America, which were, of course, relatively young and often still struggling to find legitimate forms of governance. Later *modernismo* did refocus on the Latin American experience, and even the *vanguardia* could be understood in terms of an embracing of modernity in the new Latin America – but the most famous and substantial novels of the earlier decades of the new century were those that sought specifically to capture Latin American reality and wrestle, more or less directly, with the implications of the direction that reality appeared to be taking.[2]

Indigenism

One manifestation of a concern about the lack of societal cohesion in the new nations was Indigenism. As has been seen, concern for the plight of the Indian, who had been mistreated and marginalized rather than incorporated into collective national projects, was already present in Matto de Turner's *Aves sin nido* from the nineteenth century. A number of notable indigenous novels appeared in the early twentieth century. Though not always impressive at a literary level, these novels do display key concerns of the time and paved the way for a more powerful brand of Neo-Indigenist literature later in the century (see chapter 3). Most concentrate on the brutality meted out to the Indians, accenting in particular their removal from their lands by corrupt landowners often in connivance with foreign (i.e. US) interests. The best of this type is probably Jorge Icaza's (Ecuador, 1906–78) *Huasipungo* from 1934 (though an earlier foundational example of the genre would be Bolivian Alcides Arguedas' [1879–1946] *Raza de bronce* ['Race of Bronze', 1919]). Peruvian Ciro Alegría (1909–67), in 1941, takes a similar but at the same time rather different tack in his *El mundo es ancho y ajeno* ('Broad and Alien is the World'). The difference is the (for today's tastes rather mawkish) accent on the ideal nature of the Indian way of life. The indigenous Andean community of Rumi, though affected by the outside world, is essentially presented as a repository of traditional Indian values. As with *Raza de bronce* and *Huasipungo*, land ownership is central, but here there is a predominance of lengthy lyrical passages bringing out the harmonious relationship between the Indian and nature. The wise community elder Rosendo Maqui, for instance, is portrayed as virtually indistinguishable from his natural surroundings:

Tenía el cuerpo nudoso y cetrino como el lloque – palo contorsionado y durísimo –, porque era un poco vegetal, un poco hombre, un poco piedra. . . . Tras las duras colinas de los pómulos brillaban los ojos, oscuros lagos quietos. Las cejas eran una crestería. Podría afrimarse que el Adán americano fue plasmado según su geografía; que las fuerzas de la tierra, de tan enérgicas, eclosionaron en un hombre con rasgos de montañas. En sus sienes nevaba como en las de Urpillau.[3]

(His body was knotty and olive-coloured like a *lloque* – a very hard and contorted piece of wood –, because he was part plant, part man, part stone. . . . Behind the hard hills of his cheekbones shone his eyes, those dark, placid lakes. His eyebrows were snowcapped peaks. One could say that the South American Adam was moulded from his geography; that the strength of the earth, so energetic was it, hatched a man with the characteristics of mountains. Over his forehead, his hair snowed as on the mountains of Urpillau.)

When the natives are dispossessed of their land in the name of progress by the greedy landowner Don Alvaro Amenábar, who wants the Indians only as a cheap labour force for his mines, the destruction of their community is described as a natural cataclysm: 'ahí estaba el pueblo comunero, agrario y pastoril, hijo de la tierra, enraizado en ella durante siglos y que ahora sentía, como un árbol, el dramático estrecimiento del descuaje' ('so there was the community of people, agrarian and pastoral, sons of the earth, rooted in it for centuries, and who now felt, like a tree, the dramatic shudder of uprooting') (p. 224). This, of course, is an inversion of Sarmiento's notion of Civilization and Barbarism. The indigenous community is an embodiment of a natural form of civilization based on harmony and collectivity on which violence and disorder is wrought by a bogus cult of 'progress'. The ending returns us to the pessimism of Alcides Arguedas and Icaza, when the remaining Indians are wiped out by army machine guns – a reminder of the vicious connivance of state and oligarchy in a travesty of the ideal of civilization.

The difficulty with a novel like *El mundo es ancho y ajeno* is the process of external idealization of Indians on the one hand, and demonization of landowners and politicians on the other, that tends to undermine the attempt to offer a realistic and therefore persuasive account of injustice. This limitation would have two effects in the future: the growth of a new kind of Indigenism that would seek to recreate the indigenous experience from the inside and offer therefore a rather less helpless picture of the indigenous people; and a more generalized rejection of Latin American realism as fundamentally misguided or misleading, something which would ultimately result in the triumph of the New Novel. The problem with writers like Alegría was that they were fundamentally outsiders, from the educated white middle classes, and thus prone to stereotypical or simplistic representations of reality. This outsider status was to be a factor in all the great Latin American Regionalist narratives of the early twentieth century, of which *El mundo es ancho y ajeno* is itself a rather weak late example (as well as forming part of an Indigenist tradition). Regionalism, as we shall see, was the major phenomenon in fiction in the first part of the twentieth century. And while it aimed to document realistically national realities, its concern with promoting a particular kind of agenda for the nation led to many contradictions. The history of mainstream Latin American fiction in the early twentieth century will become a history, in other words, of flawed classics.

Regionalism

With regard to prose fiction, Regionalism became the dominant narrative form in the first few decades of the twentieth century. It is actually referred to by a variety of names: also, for example, as the novel of the land or *novela de la tierra*, as autochthonous fiction or sometimes *criollista* fiction. In Brazil, meantime, it is sometimes associated with a specific region, the drought-stricken north-eastern *sertão* or backlands, and tends to be more self-contained and identified largely with a kind of 1930s Neorealism focusing on human suffering.[4] The emergence of the regional novel has traditionally been explained in both literary and social terms. It has been seen, in part, as a reaction against what was perceived as an inherited European tradition of Romanticism and, perhaps later, official Realism. On the one hand, writers sought to escape the Romantic model by concentrating on what was uniquely Latin American (hence the regional emphasis). On the other hand, they equally wished to avoid the Dickensian or Galdosian model of Realism which seemed to deal mainly with urban life (again, it was the regions that marked Latin America's difference from Europe). As has been seen, none the less, in practice much Romantic fiction in Latin America was very much concerned with national realities. And, at the same time, Regionalist writing did aim to be realistic in its documentation of regional ways of life.

Regionalism can probably be more usefully understood as a continuation and more explicit refinement of the national and continental post-Independence concerns of the nineteenth century in the form of novels for which there was something more of a literate, educated, national public (though underdeveloped in comparison to, say, north-western Europe). In fact, regional fictions tend usually to be very much wrapped up in expressing or challenging (both consciously and unconsciously) the Sarmientan notion of Civilization and Barbarism. In other words, they continued to be manifestations of aspirations or anxieties about the new social order that was still uncertainly evolving in the young nations after Independence. And the truth of the matter is that these novels were full of tensions and contradictions, centring principally on the struggle by representatives of an essentially urban or upper-middle-class intelligentsia to capture, rehabilitate or offer counsel for the lifestyles and values of the gauchos, Indians and peasantry. The blueprint for national identity that they promoted was at heart an extremely uneasy mixture of 'civilization' and 'barbarism', city and countryside, progress and tradition, liberalism and conservatism. Though Regionalism would later be seen as emblematic of the 'traditional' literature against which the self-consciously 'modern' New Narrative measured itself, the phenomenon was really another instance of the crisis of modernity that had been playing itself out since Independence. The peculiarity of Regionalism (and perhaps of Latin American literature as a whole) is the awkward attempt to envisage a modern, just and viable state via the forging of an essential identity based on the past, on local traditions and identities that are fundamentally in conflict with the very programme of modernity.[5]

The novel of the Mexican Revolution

The real flourishing of Regionalism came in the 1920s, but one of the earliest examples of it is a novel that some critics might not even classify as regional fiction in the strict sense, and that is *Los de abajo* ('The Underdogs', 1915) by the Mexican Mariano Azuela (1873–1952). This work does focus on the regions and the peasantry, but also on what was a major instance of a social and political reawakening in the subcontinent, the Mexican Revolution. This began in 1911 as a rebellion against the dictatorship of Porfirio Díaz but soon degenerated into factional strife between rival revolutionary groups. *Los de abajo* deals with a short period of the fighting phase of the Revolution, roughly between 1913 and 1915. It is set against the background of the struggle against the corrupt regime of Victoriano Huerta and the subsequent collapse of the Revolution into a bitter power struggle between Venustiano Carranza and the bandit leader Pancho Villa, culminating in the disastrous defeat of Villa after the battle of Celaya in April 1915. In the novel a (fictional) peasant farmer Demetrio Macías becomes embroiled in the Revolution after a row with a local landlord or *cacique* and gradually rises to the position of an army leader. He is described as playing a triumphant role in the famous battle of Zacatecas (24 June 1914), which marked the defeat of Huerta, but then is unwittingly sucked into the factional strife between Carranza and Villa. Having made the fateful decision to side with Villa, Demetrio and his men are wiped out in the final chapter in the very same canyon where they scored their first victory at the beginning of the novel. What this pattern of chaos and circularity brings out is the futility of the Revolution, which is seen as failing to achieve any of its original ideals.

The failure of the Revolution, or, more concretely, the idea of the Revolution betrayed, came to be a stock theme of Mexican literature (and one can in fact speak of the novel of the Mexican Revolution as a genre or sub-genre of its own[6]). The thinking of liberal intellectuals was that the Revolution became little more than a senseless bloodbath and that it simply opened the country up to a new breed of parasitical opportunists, who used revolutionary rhetoric to advance their own careers and interests. Much of *Los de abajo* dwells on the violence of war, whose conditions of lawlessness make the conflict a magnet for the worst types in society. As Demetrio's band grows it attracts an increasingly unsavoury following: most notably Venancio and Codorniz, who join up to escape punishment for crimes, Pancracio and Manteca, who revel in violence, the evil whore Pintada and the psychopathic Margarito. The dehumanizing affect of war is summed up in the character of the innocent young Anastasio Montañés. In a battle scene where the sinister Pancracio and Manteca are going around finishing off the enemy wounded, 'Montañés deja caer su mano, rendido ya; en su semblante persiste su mirada dulzona, en su impasible rostro brillan la ingenuidad del niño y la amoralidad del chacal' ('Montañés, exhausted, let his hand fall; in his countenance there remained his look of sweet gentleness, while on his impassive face there shone the naivety of a child and the amorality of a jackal').[7] War has made an innocent man capable of killing like a wild beast. Most of the characters undergo a similar process of moral decline, including the heroic Demetrio, who, after Zacatecas, becomes – briefly – a directionless looter, womanizer and drunk. However, the novel lays the blame not on the fundamentally decent peasants, but on middle-class opportunists, emblematized in the figure of Luis Cervantes.

Luis Cervantes is a middle-class journalist who latches on to Demetrio and his band, successfully guiding them towards integration into the mainstream of the Revolution. Oddly enough, Cervantes is the only mouthpiece in the novel for the revolutionary ideals of justice and fairness. In part this is a device (repeatedly employed) to throw into relief the ignorance of the peasants, who have no real idea why they are under arms, thus underscoring the theme of the pointlessness of the war and the lack of a convincing ideological motivation in its protagonists. But Cervantes is equally part of the same problem. His rhetoric is empty sloganizing and he exploits his connection with Demetrio's winning streak to gain influence and fill his pockets. This is the real tragedy of the Revolution: the way its ideals have been ruthlessly betrayed to favour the interests of a new emerging elite, leaving the poor peasants (as the ending shows) no better off than they originally were. This viewpoint is summed up by the disillusioned idealist Alberto Solís at Zacatecas: '¡Qué chasco . . . si los que venimos a ofrecer todo nuestro entusiasmo, nuestra misma vida por derribar a un miserable asesino, resultásemos los obreros de un enorme pedestal donde pudieran levantarse cien o doscientos mil monstruos de la misma especie!' ('What a let down . . . if those of us who come here to offer up our enthusiasm, our very life even, to bring down one wretched murderer, end up being the builders of an enormous pedestal upon which one or two hundred thousand monsters of the same sort can rise up!') (p. 135). This is a key moment in the novel. Solís is describing the battle to Cervantes, who, typically, is avoiding the trouble and taking cover behind some fortifications. At this point Solís is shot dead by a sniper's bullet, while Cervantes saves his skin. Thus the moment of the supposed triumph of the Revolution (the glorious battle of Zacatecas) actually coincides with the symbolic death of idealism (Solís) and the survival of opportunism (Cervantes). The episode is a superbly economical commentary on the failure and betrayal of the Revolution.

The seemingly despairing vision of *Los de abajo* has obvious echoes of Sarmiento and his followers. During their orgies of looting, the peasants are seen mindlessly destroying symbols of a carefully built up civilization. In one town, the men smash to bits objects they see as pointless: a typewriter, fine crystal and porcelain, candelabras, vases and statuettes (pp. 127–8). Elsewhere, a peasant burns books while the syphilitic prostitute he is with tears up a copy of Dante's *Divine Comedy* (p. 143). Throughout the novel, nature imagery presents the Revolution as an unstoppable cataclysm tearing down the foundations of civilized life. Even worse, Solís comes close to suggesting that the cataclysm is a result of the inherently barbaric nature of the Mexican people, a 'raza irredenta' ('godforsaken race') (p. 126) as he sees them: 'la psicología de nuestra raza, condensada en dos palabras: ¡robar, matar!' ('the entire psychology of our race can be summed up in two words: robbing and killing!') (p. 135). It is widely assumed that Solís is a mouthpiece for Azuela, but, of course, there is no reason why this should be necessarily so. Solís' pessimism is extreme and the view of the ordinary people put across by Azuela is often favourable, at the very least ambiguous. The novel's ending, for instance – despite its frustrating allusions to fruitless circularity – simultaneously belittles and exalts Demetrio and his men. Their gallant fight to the death is played out against a background of breathtaking nature imagery. The continuity of nature stresses the irrelevance of their acts in the ongoing wider scheme of things, yet the framing of those acts against a pure white mountain range and a sumptuous, cathedral-like canyon elevates them to epically heroic proportions. The point is that the exalted noble values of the great cause have been belittled by the sordid realities of the conflict. Yet the problem with this position is – in part – the inevitable one of a liberal perspective on revolution, for violent upheaval is an unavoidable component of the revolutionary process. The impression is given that the well-meaning Azuela does not really fully grasp the nature of the revolutionary forces that have been set in motion and continues to cling to a rather conservative notion of civilized values.

This ambiguity at the heart of the novel cannot be separated from issues of style and form. If regional novels later were to become identified with a kind of simplistic, black-and-white social realism, then *Los de abajo* appears to demonstrate that such a view is to some extent problematic. Though grit often mixes with lyricism, it does adopt a fundamentally realist approach: yet the uncertainty in point of view (coupled with a fragmentary or episodic structural pattern that recreates a sense of the chaos of war) anticipates – albeit palely – future developments in narrative. A realist mode was certainly becoming the main narrative force in Latin America in the early twentieth century, but it also contained the seeds of its own transcendence even in its earliest stages.

Novels of the land: the *llano* and the *pampa*

Similar tensions can be identified in the heyday of Regionalism in the 1920s. What are generally regarded as the two greatest regional novels appeared in this decade: *Doña Bárbara* (1929) by Venezuela's Rómulo Gallegos (1884–1969) and *Don Segundo Sombra* (1926) by Argentina's Ricardo Güiraldes (1886–1927). Both are authentic 'novels of the land', dealing with life in the interior plains or grasslands of the Venezuelan *llano* or the Argentine *pampa*. Conceptually, they are probably best read in reverse chronological order (chronology in an area as vast, varied and developmentally uneven as Latin America can often be misleading). *Doña Bárbara* is often considered the classic Spanish American novel, but nowadays it probably reads as unsophisticated both as literature and as social commentary. As a work of art, it has its dramatic moments, but is really, for today's tastes, rather tedious and long-winded in its lengthy technical and costumbrist depictions of the practices of the *llaneros* or plainsmen. Moreover, at the level of ideas, its message of progress can, in fact, be seen as rather regressive and failing to advance much beyond nineteenth-century positivism[8] or stereotypical readings of Sarmiento. The problem is that, in an echo of the pessimism of Alberto Solís in *Los de abajo*, Gallegos appears to believe in the idea of an *alma de la raza* (soul of the race or people), a national mentality predisposed towards barbarism. This, of course, is most prevalent in the rustic interior and needs to be tamed by the importation of civilized, city-based values. So, in the novel, the hero is the educated, city-raised Santos Luzardo, who returns to his rural family estate, Altamira. There he confronts and eventually defeats barbarism in the shape of the backward, evil landowner Doña

Bárbara, who has sought to rule the region tyrannically from her estate, El Miedo. The symbolism is painfully obvious, the names of the protagonists and their properties connoting 'saintly light' and 'high ideals' on the one hand, and 'barbarism' and 'fear' on the other. Decent, progressive values rooted in the European Enlightenment are the only way to eliminate the dark threat of a retrograde native tradition.

Bárbara is described at one stage as a 'personificación de los tiempos que corrían',[9] a personification of the times. Gallegos was himself an educator, politician and future president of the Republic, and his notion of barbarism could be taken as the absence of good govern-ment (which was really what Sarmiento was saying about Rosas) and therefore a very specific commentary on the dictatorship of Juan Vicente Gómez (1908–35). Though initially quite progressive, Gómez would probably have been seen by Gallegos as having done little to combat the forces of barbarism and – with the passive support of an inert or abulic landowning class, also satirized in the novel – exposing the country to the rapacious clutches of foreign interests (represented by the villainous North American named, none too subtly, Mr Dánger). Thus Santos, in such a reading, would be the embodiment of a new, more intellectual generation that would bring order and prosperity to the nation. Indeed, what is interesting about the novel is its degree of emphasis on Santos' practical efforts to manage and modernize the local environment and processes of production. This undermines the notion of the *alma de la raza* as the source of the country's ills, because it suggests that the problem will simply go away with proper social and economic reform. Once more the attitude to the supposedly 'barbaric' interior is profoundly ambiguous. 'La llanura es bella y terrible a la vez' '(the plains are beautiful and terrible at the same time') (p. 66), we are told; and even Bárbara, the incarnation of barbarism, has 'algo de salvaje, bello y terrible a la vez' ('something of the savage, beauti-ful and terrible at the same time') (p. 36). Moreover, to complicate matters even further, Santos himself repeatedly feels the heady pull of the 'barbaric' way of life and is only ultimately able to defeat his enemies by adopting their own violent methods.

This ambiguity may suggest that the realist model is more subtle than later generations would appreciate. Or, perhaps more likely, it may suggest Gallegos' confused thinking. But Gallegos may be occupying much more of a middle ground than a superficial reading might suggest. From this point of view, Santos' relationship with the young Marisela is crucial. She is a girl who has been abandoned to nature and could be taken to represent the *alma de la raza* in a pure, uncontaminated state, untouched by either 'civilization' or 'barbarism'. Though Santos does to some extent civilize Marisela by education, manners and even appropriately feminine clothes and hairstyle, there is also a strong sense that what he learns fundamentally is not to impose on her some artificial notion of civilization but to bring out the positive qualities latent within her and the rural culture from which she hails. In effect Marisela teaches the civilizer 'su verdadera obra, porque la suya no podía ser exterminar el mal a sangre y fuego, sino descubrir, aquí y allá, las fuentes ocultas de la bondad de su tierra y de su gente' ('his real task, for his could not be to wipe out evil with blood and fire, but instead to uncover the hidden sources of goodness in his people and his land') (p. 264).[10]

Even more ambiguous (or confused) is *Don Segundo Sombra*, though in a rather inverse way to that of *Doña Bárbara*. Güiraldes' novel seems to be a complete rejection of traditional understandings of Sarmiento and instead marks the climax of gauchesque writing's process of rehabilitation of the gaucho that began back with the *Martín Fierro* (see chapter 1). The eponymous hero Don Segundo Sombra is the incarnation of the noble and free spirit of the nomadic gaucho and of all that is best in the gaucho tradition. At one level, the novel is in fact a kind of catalogue of gaucho values and customs, with copious descriptions of the skills of the herdsman, his characteristics of stoicism and resilience, and his colourful pastimes and entertainments. Don Segundo is the embodiment of the gaucho *par excellence*. So much so, that right from his very first extraordinary, shadowy appearance from out of the darkness, he comes across as 'una sombra, algo que pasa y es más una idea que un ser' ('a shadow, something which passes by and is more of an idea than a human being as such').[11] Similarly, the novel ends with him returning whence he came, horse and rider silhouetted against the horizon: 'aquello que se alejaba era más una idea que un hombre' ('that thing that was heading away was more of an idea than a man') (p. 185). The point is that Don Segundo is the essence of the gaucho legend, and, by extension, the expression of those essential national virtues that should form a kind of mythical basis for Argentine identity.

In this regard, it is important that the gaucho is seen largely through the eyes of his young protégé, and the novel's narrator, Fabio Cáceres.

Don Segundo is, in other words, a projection of the ideals or dreams of the younger generation which Fabio represents. The focus of the novel is really on the young Fabio's apprenticeship in the whys and wherefores of the gaucho way at the hands of his older mentor. But at the end of the novel, the so far anonymous narrator is named for the first time as the son of a landowner and is returned to the family estate to claim his inheritance. Thus the novel's main contention seems to be that the new generation of leaders must base their beliefs and practices on traditional gaucho lore and custom, that is on that which is authentically national. As Don Segundo advises Fabio, as he leaves behind the cowboy life to prepare for his future position at the head of the social and economic powerhouse of the ranch economy: 'si sos gaucho en de veras, no has de mudar, porque andequiera que vayas, irás con tu alma por delante como madrina'e tropilla' ('if you're a true gaucho, you'll never have to change, because wherever you go in life, you'll always have your gaucho soul right there before you just as the head of the herd does') (p. 176). By the end, Fabio is becoming an educated and enlightened man, yet true to the lessons he has learned from Don Segundo. Indeed the very narrative we are reading is testament to this process: written by the adult Fabio, it encapsulates the gaucho national tradition but within the framework of a sophisticated and stylized account. The text itself becomes a kind of metaphor for the way forward for the nation.

However, the oscillation between stylistic panache and the rough-and-tumble of rustic life gives something of an awkward tone to the novel and returns us once again to the realm of ambiguity and con-tradiction. Fabio's sometimes precious language reveals the presence behind the tale of Güiraldes himself – a very literary, cosmopolitan, French-educated, landowning aristocrat with an enthusiasm for the way of life of the gauchos. The fact is that by the time *Don Segundo Sombra* was written, the gauchos had effectively disappeared as a distinct social group and the *pampa* had been transformed by agricul-tural modernization, roads, railways and the influx of technically skilled and entrepreneurial European immigrants (this educational or attitudinal 'whitening' being part of the legacy of the thinking of Sarmiento and others). The ideal world that Güiraldes conjures up simply did not exist. And so the novel can be seen as deeply con-servative rather than radical, another nostalgic nationalist elegy for a bygone era at a time of change, and an expression of the anxiety of a traditional ruling class on the brink of a new age of modernization, urbanization, immigration and foreign influence.

Indeed the glorification of the gaucho as model for national identity is not only supremely vague but also potentially quite dangerous. A revealing (if probably unconsciously so) episode in this respect is when the otherwise idealized Don Segundo intervenes in a quarrel so as to prompt a young man into a knife-fight, resulting in the gruesome death of his opponent and the destruction of the young man's life.[12] The sheer horror of the episode and the astounded reaction of Fabio and the onlookers should sound alarm bells for the alert reader, pointing up the unsuitability of the lawless and violence-prone gaucho as a basis for national identity. Despite the mythical forging of a striking national icon, the impact of books like *Don Segundo Sombra* may ultimately have made a less than distinguished contribution to a culture that would for many decades be characterized by populism, bossism, fanaticism, machismo and dictatorship.

Jungle narratives and glimpses of the modern

If *Doña Bárbara* and *Don Segundo Sombra*'s examination of identity implies – in different ways – a not altogether convincing desire to cling to a notion of order, an earlier example of Regionalism, dealing with the much more chaotic world of the jungle, seems to emphasize the inevitability of the opposite. This is the Colombian José Eustasio Rivera's (1889–1928) work of 1924, *La vorágine* ('The Vortex'). Of all the regional novels discussed, this, in spite of its vintage, is probably the closest to the kind of New Narrative that would emerge later in the twentieth century in Latin America. Paradoxically, in some ways this is because it is an early novel and seems at times rather messy in its mixture of intersecting trends and influences. But its portrait of its protagonist, Arturo Cova, as he is sucked into and consumed by the vortex of the jungle and of his own unbalanced mind, is remarkably compelling.

Ostensibly, this is a documentary novel of social protest exposing the desperate conditions of rubber workers in the Amazon jungle. At this level, it is powerful and effective, but any straight sense of documentary realism is undermined by the constant changes in direction, the inconsistencies of character and, above all, the complex psychological rendering of Cova. A city man from Bogotá, he runs off to the jungle with his lover Alicia to escape a stifling world of conservatism. However, the journey to the interior proves to be far from liberating. Even before full immersion into the horrific scenario of *cauchero* (rubber tapper) abuse, entry to the jungle is a nightmarish experience of near Satanic madness in which nature is presented as a kind of devouring monster.[13] Leaving behind the open plains, Cova is absorbed into a thick, matted world without horizons or the possibility of orientation, a world of 'laberintos', 'enfermizas penumbras', a 'cementerio enorme donde te pudres y resucitas', a place where 'mi espíritu sólo se aviene con lo inestable que soporta el peso de tu perpetuidad' ('labyrinths', 'sickly shadows', an 'enormous cemetery in which you rot and are recreated', a place where 'my spirit can only reconcile itself with the instability which is supported by the weight of your perpetuity') (pp. 117–18).

This is a much more visceral take on Civilization and Barbarism. Whereas Gallegos will deal with humans' controlling of nature, Rivera here shows the irresponsibility of men in the face of nature (as seen in the exploitation by the rubber tappers) and the tremendous power of nature over men (as reflected in the fate of the *caucheros* and Cova himself). But what is really interesting from a literary point of view is the way it becomes almost impossible to distinguish the effects of the jungle upon Cova from his own increasingly crazed descriptions of it. Far from an easy social realism, this novel is foreshadowing a future type of narrative in which external reality will be presented as inseparable from mental perceptions of it.

All of which leads us to one final key transitional figure, Latin America's first major writer of short stories, the Uruguayan Horacio Quiroga (1878–1937). Again, chronology is not the issue here (many of his best stories predate the regional novels considered here): rather it is the existence in the early twentieth century of a series of sometimes complementary, sometimes sharply differentiated, approaches or frames of mind spread across a very large, unequal, social and geographical area. Quiroga is interesting precisely because his writing style is an intriguing blend of realism, *modernista* influences, a nascent literature of fantasy and a rather dark world view that portends the crisis of faith of a more self-conscious modernity. His most famous stories are probably those which can be most easily identified with the trend of Regionalism, namely those set in the tropical or jungle areas of the Chaco or around Misiones in the interior (both places where Quiroga himself settled). However, unlike the works of Gallegos, Güiraldes and even Rivera (whose novel contains much reflection on Colombian identity), Quiroga does not seem to be directly engaged with questions of national identity. His contribution is a more general one to *criollista* literature in that it expresses a mentality that is concerned with the regional interior and the opportunities and threats that it presents. His stories, in fact, are usually about individualistic pioneers or frontiersmen who seek a new life for themselves in the underexplored regions, rather than about the conscious mapping of national territorial identities.

Though these stories are traditionally realistic in their setting of human activity against an external natural environment, they also reveal many ambivalences. For a start, the nature stories often have two different main focuses. They tend first to emphasize the arrogance and puniness of human beings in the face of the awesome power of nature. In the story 'Anaconda' the natural balance of nature is upset when humans build an institute in the jungle designed to find antidotes to snake venom, thus altering the usual order of things. Told from the snakes' point of view, 'la presencia del Hombre' ('the presence of Man') is equated with the phrase 'mal asunto' ('bad news'), and 'Hombre y Devastación son sinónimos desde tiempo inmemorial en el Pueblo entero de los Animales' ('Man and Devastation have been synonymous in the whole Animal kingdom since time immemorial').[14] And even stories like 'A la deriva' ('Drifting') or 'El hombre muerto' ('The Dead Man'), which seem to suggest the role of chance or fate in the death of men, accentuate the smugness and carelessness of man in the face of nature as the main cause of death.

Yet if some stories are devastatingly critical of human presumptuousness in the jungle, others express tremendous admiration for those who struggle courageously against the limitations imposed by the natural world. Both elements are present sketchily in the two stories just mentioned, but can be seen more obviously in tales like 'Los fabricantes de carbón' ('The Charcoal Makers') and 'En la noche' ('In the Night'): in the first, two tenacious men quietly pursue a scheme to build a charcoal-making furnace despite facing insurmountable odds due to local conditions; in the second, a vulgar and grasping woman shows unheralded reserves of heroism when she rows her husband, who is close to death after being bitten by a stingray, to safety in the impossibly treacherous conditions of the Paraná River by night ('qué cantidad de ideal hay en la entraña misma de la acción' [p. 126] concludes the narrator, telling us that heroism has nothing to do with beliefs or ideals but with the actions human beings perform).

Taken as a whole, then, Quiroga's jungle stories offer a kaleidoscopic picture of pioneer life in the backwoods (a clear realist strain), but also display a degree of uncertainty about human nature that betrays some chinks in the realist armoury. Indeed, though it is sometimes claimed that Quiroga's tales reveal a clear separation between individual and external reality, this is often not the case, as, for instance, in the aforementioned 'A la deriva'. Here, as another jungle bite victim drifts down the river to his death, the descriptions of the landscape are clearly not neutral but a complex amalgam of character and implied narratorial perspective. Two passages can be compared. One begins with the phrase 'El Paraná corre allí en el fondo de una inmensa hoya, cuyas paredas, altas de cien metros, encajonan fúnebremente el río' ('The Paraná around there runs down into a deep hole-like basin, whose sides, about a hundred metres high, funereally wall in the river like a coffin'), continuing with a description of the surroundings using words such as 'negros bloques', 'la eterna muralla lúgubre' and 'un silencio de muerte' ('black blocks', 'an eternal lugubrious wall' and 'the silence of death') (p. 158). A second, following the protagonist's speculation that he may soon reach safety, describes the sky opening up into a 'pantalla de oro y el río se había coloreado también' ('a screen of gold and the river had filled up with colour too'), while 'el monte dejaba caer sobre el río su frescura crepuscular en penetrantes efluvios de azahar y miel silvestre' ('the woodland allowed its crepuscular freshness to tumble down on to the river with penetrating fragrances of orange blossom and wild honey') (p. 158). These passages are clearly more than straight description of landscape. The first actually seems to be a narratorial projection of inevitable death, in contrast with the second, which (with its sudden bursts of colour, freshness, fertility and life) may be taken as an ironized manifestation of the main character's futile hopes of salvation. Whatever the interpretation, the boundary between internal perception and external reality has been transgressed.

What the above also seems to indicate is that Quiroga's stories are not just about man and his environment, but also about the very nature of life and death. The prevalence of death in his stories is a feature much commented upon, and is often related to the extraordinarily tragic circumstances of his own life (apart from failed pioneering enterprises and love affairs, his life was marred by a bizarre series of mishaps including various accidental deaths and suicides). This overlaying of pessimism in his stories may mark Quiroga as a transitional figure, concerned not just about observable external reality but about the interior and unknown world of the psyche too. In fact he is compared to Edgar Allan Poe as much as he is to Rudyard Kipling, and many of Quiroga's tales are macabre stories of horror and madness, such as, for instance, 'La gallina degollada' ('The Beheaded Hen'), 'El almohadón de plumas' ('The Feather Pillow') and 'La miel silvestre' ('Wild Honey'). These stories deal with: a group of subnormal children who mimic the bestial pleasure of seeing the blood drained from a chicken's neck by killing their little sister; a woman driven to delirium and death by a monstrous creature residing in her pillow; and the grisly demise of a man, paralysed by wild bees' honey yet fully conscious, who is slowly eaten to death by carnivorous ants. Quiroga, then, is no ordinary Regionalist and no ordinary realist. Nor, of course, is he a modernist in the Anglo-American sense. What his work does is to remind us of the varied and transitional nature of narrative in early twentieth-century Latin America. As will be seen in the next chapter, at the same time as the purported social realist ethos of Regionalism was coming to prominence, other types of experimental literary stirrings could be perceived and the stage was being set for the rise of the New Novel, something that would change perceptions of Latin American literature forever.

CHAPTER 3

The Rise of the New Narrative

In terms of international recognition, the most important development in the whole of Latin American literature was the growth of the so-called New Novel or New Narrative (*nueva novela* or *nueva narrativa*) in – roughly – the 1940s and 1950s, culminating in the spectacular success of what came to be known as the Boom (*el boom*) in the 1960s and beyond. Most commonly, the New Novel is explained as the reaction against or rejection of conventional realism. The notion is that Latin American fiction had been dominated by a sort of simplistic social realism (as in the regional novel, for example), which, while seeking to offer an objective document of reality, was actually steering the reader towards a rather narrow and unambiguous (usually social) interpretation of reality. The danger was that, given the assumption of the validity of realism, a novelist's distortions could take on the quality of truth, with omniscient third-person narration placing the reader in the position of passive recipient of that dubious truth.

The New Novel was seen to question the key underlying assumptions of traditional realism: that reality was straightforward or even comprehensible; and that reality could ever be captured easily or accurately in writing. This sceptical attitude to reality and literature – often linked to the idea of a general crisis of modern times emanating from the loss of foundational beliefs and certainties rooted in Western and Christian values – led to a new type of fiction. Previously, an orderly world view was reflected in an orderly style of fiction. Now, a more uncertain, less meaningful, perhaps even chaotic perception of reality was reflected in a narrative form which sought to recreate the complex, contradictory, fluid, ambiguous or even plain unintelligible nature of reality. Hence the New Narrative would come to be characterized by a range of 'difficult' narrative techniques which demanded a more active role from the reader, shaking him or her out of acquiescent passivity and into adopting a more active and engaged role in the construction or reconstruction of the narrative itself.[1]

This is the theory at least. But though the above is a useful guide for understanding the thinking behind the New Narrative, the vision of realism on which it is predicated is in many ways a notional one. In practice, realism in Latin America was more varied and ambiguous than imaginary versions of it might suggest. One has but to think of Quiroga's playing with perception and reality, the fragmentary structure and shifting portrayal of the peasantry in *Los de abajo*, the simultaneous repulsion from and attraction to barbarism in Gallegos, or the anxious conservatism behind the modern reconception of the gaucho and identity in *Don Segundo Sombra*. Indeed, what may have happened (justifying the inverse chronology of the previous chapter) is that, as Regionalism continued, it became increasingly staid, predictable and formulaic, so that later writers began to react against poorer novels like, say, *El mundo es ancho y ajeno*, and project their defects backwards on to a perceived realist-Regionalist tradition. Moreover, other things were happening at the same time as national and regional novels were coming to prominence. Movements such as *modernismo* and the *vanguardia* were radically challenging conventional ideas of what literature was for or about, and a new type of writing – sometimes more public, sometimes more subterranean, sometimes more popular, sometimes more specialist – was growing in parallel with the thrust to realism. In other words, the New Novel does not just come from nowhere as a modern literary reaction against tradition. It has its roots in the past, despite its obsession with the idea of the new.

Modernismo

Modernismo was traditionally seen specifically as a phenomenon of the Latin American *fin de siècle* (though influential in Spain), focused primarily on poetry (hence it is a quite different term to modernism in the Anglo-American sense). With its influences lying in the escapist dimension of European Romanticism and, more particularly, in the *l'art pour l'art* or 'art for art's sake' mentality of French Symbolist or Parnassian poetry, the movement was seen as a reaction against national and patriotic writing which banished literariness to a subordinate role, and therefore put the emphasis on aesthetic qualities of style and mood. The quintessential *modernista* work would probably be the collection of poems, *Prosas profanas* (1896, published 1901), by the Nicaraguan Rubén Darío (1867–1916). However, later criticism has looked beyond the apparent superficiality of Darío and the *modernistas*, and seen them as marking the first real steps in the creation of a sense of literary modernity in Latin America.[2] The sense of escapism is now seen as an expression of a crisis of faith in the wake of new philosophical ideas from Europe (for example, those of Schopenhauer) questioning conventional belief systems and the positivist emphasis on social progress, which seemed to emphasize the material over the spiritual and encourage the breakdown of social patternings via technological change, urbanization, immigration and social mobility.

Oddly enough, though, *modernismo* would have effects that many of its poet practitioners might not have predicted. Their poetry really embodied a yearning for an alternative order, but their emphasis on absence of order would encourage the next generation of poets to concentrate on the disintegration of any concept of harmony. More generally, in freeing language from the obligation to reflect social reality (the most far-reaching consequence of *modernismo* for Latin American letters), *modernismo* paved the way for what was to become the basic tenet of the later New Narrative: the idea that language cannot effectively describe reality because reality itself is at best problematic or at worst incomprehensible and meaningless.

Contemporary criticism has tried to assert the importance of *modernista* fiction.[3] However, the fact probably remains that, while critical archaeology can unearth many examples of the *modernista* novel, it was *modernista* poetry and the general aesthetic surrounding it which marked the really significant influence in the developing of a more modernist (in the wider Anglo-American sense of a radical break with tradition via innovative writing) direction in Latin American narrative. The same is probably true of the *vanguardia*. Experimental avant-garde poems and other writings flourished as the twentieth century progressed, especially in the 1920s and 1930s. This was under the influence of European trends (brought across, in particular, by

European magazines), and such creative activity often centred on new Latin American literary groups or magazines, usually in the major urban metropolises. In Brazil, European aesthetics were much more publicly embraced and gave rise to that country's own version of the avant-garde – to complicate matters, also known as *modernismo*: this began with the famous 'Semana de Arte Moderna' ('Week of Modern Art') which took place in São Paulo in February 1922, and led to a version of the creative arts (especially poetry) characterized by an intriguing blend of futurist and primitivist trends appropriate to Brazilian intellectuals' attempts to reconcile modernity with ethnic roots. There were vanguard novelists in Latin America (though classification of them sometimes tends towards vagueness)[4], but, again, it was the general parallel and mainly poetic aesthetic running alongside Regionalism that contributed to longer-term change.

No *modernista* novel really stood the test of time, though the most famous – and also one of the latest – is *La Gloria de don Ramiro* ('The Glory of Don Ramiro', 1908) by Enrique Larreta (Argentina, 1873–1961). It brings out the *modernistas'* familiar fascination with escapism and the exotic: set in far-off sixteenth-century Spain, it deals with, amongst other things in a fairly lively plot, a man's only part-reluctant induction into the sensual ambience of Moorish culture. Perhaps the most striking feature of this historical setting is the apparent break with Spanish American referentiality. This is less the case in the earlier novels of Manuel Díaz Rodríguez (Venezuela, 1868–1927), whose *Idolos rotos* ('Broken Idols', 1901) and *Sangre patricia* ('Patrician Blood', 1902) deal with the corrosive moral affects of modern commerce and entrepreneurialism. Such ideas are an echo of José Enrique Rodó's (Uruguay, 1871–1917) influential essay of 1900, *Ariel*, which uses the figures of Caliban and Ariel from Shakespeare's *The Tempest* to oppose the crass materialism of North American capital to the ideal spirit of wisdom, beauty and spirituality to be transmitted by Spanish American intellectuals.[5] However, such a position could also be taken as a sign of decadence and evasion, a fleeing from reality. In fact, the main appeal of Díaz Rodríguez's novels is their sumptuous *modernista* prose rather than their content. The same could be said of Pedro Prado's (Chile, 1886–1952) late *modernista* novel *Alsino* (1920), which – though full of references to Chile – is a lyrical tale of a boy who sprouts wings. His death, though, with its echoes of Icarus, returns us to the theme of the failed quest for the ideal.

Modernismo was often about esoteric questing for alternative spiritual meaning, as is reflected in, for example, the fantastic tales of Leopoldo Lugones (Argentina, 1874–1938). But though flashy *modernismo* was fascinated with novelty and alternative worlds, in the end it ironically expresses the crisis of modernity (that is, scepticism and loss of faith) that was to mark so much modern literature. Unsurprisingly, Darío's last great poem, 'Lo fatal' ('The Fatal' or, perhaps, 'The Fateful') ends with despair in the face of a life in which one can never know 'adónde vamos / ni de dónde venimos' ('where we are going / nor where we have come from').[6]

Avant-garde Tendencies

The *vanguardia* or avant-garde, in Latin America as in Europe, was also based on a peculiar mixture of the exhilaration of the new and the anxiety of modernity. *Vanguardista* poetry set a tone of breaking with traditions of representation that would affect prose production alongside the broadly realist Regionalism and anticipate the later experiments of the New Narrative. There was a range of writers in the first half of the twentieth century who could be styled avant-garde in the loosest sense of the term.[7]

One of the earliest, if not the most typical, was Eduardo Barrios (Chile, 1884–1963). Though he wrote a version of a regional novel in 1948, *Gran señor y rajadiablos* ('Big Boss and the Hellraiser'), his earlier *El hermano asno* ('Brother Ass', 1922), about monks struggling with emotion, is sometimes seen as predicting the ambiguity and anti-rationality of future work by others: but the reality is that this is a rather beautifully written novel about the positive value of religion and spirituality. More obviously indebted to the avant-garde are the novels of María Luisa Bombal (Chile, 1910–80), *La última niebla* (tr. 'House of Fog', 1935) and *La amortajada* ('The Shrouded Woman', 1938). Both titles already imply a break with the aspired-to representational clarity of realism. They offer instead a psychological-cum-fantastic window on existence: in the first novel, an alienated housewife withdraws into a silent fantasy world where she invents an enigmatic lover; in the second, a dead woman tells the story of her empty life from her coffin. Even more fantastic are the eccentric stories and novellas of the Uruguayan Felisberto Hernández (1902–64) dating from the 1920s to the 1960s: in them, for example, a cigarette gets a mind of its own, a woman falls in love with a balcony, a stocking-seller makes a living by crying, and a man seeks a relationship with water-filled dolls.

The most important of these experimenting precursors of modernity is probably Argentina's Macedonio Fernández (1874–1952). The prescience of his writing is illustrated by the fact that his major work, *Museo de la Novela de la Eterna* ('Museum of the Novel of the Eternal Woman'), was not published until 1967, at the height of the Boom, though written many years earlier. Macedonio's 'novel' radically undermines conventional notions of the self and reality. Introducing what he calls the new approach of *belarte*, he eschews traditional characters and narrative forms in order to rattle the reader's sense of coherence. On top of this, the novel enjoys fifty-six prologues and an open ending, where another prologue encourages future readers to edit or rewrite the text. The aim is, via literary disorientation, to provoke in the reader 'la conmoción de la certeza de ser' ('the shaking-up of the certainty of existing') or 'el mareo de su certidumbre de ser' ('dizzying his or her sureness of existing').[8] This is remarkably similar (in tone at least) to the most radical territory of the *nueva narrativa*.

What seems to be emerging with these (in the broad sense) vanguard tendencies is an interrelated literary and existential reaction to the experience of modernity. In some ways, all Latin American literature after Sarmiento was wrestling with modernity, but now the perspective seems to have shifted from the aspiration for social and political order to a feeling of almost complete scepticism and hopelessness with regard to order as an epistemological or even onto-logical concept. If realist literary structures implied ordered values and attachment to the idea of external social reality, the new, frac-tured writing of the twentieth century was suggesting a much wider existential or metaphysical malaise, in which the very idea of reality was problematic and life itself was possibly without any fundamental meaning. This perceived shift has led in recent years to innumerable critical debates about specificity versus universality (see chapter 7), but no amount of theory or politics can alter the fact that a change in sensibility did seem to take place. As Mario Vargas Llosa famously said of the New Narrative, 'la novela deja de ser "latinoamericana", se libera de esa servidumbre' ('the novel ceases to be "Latin American", it frees itself from such servitude').[9] A number of important authors from the River Plate area will allow us to trace this trend up to its most powerful and important manifestation in the fictions of Jorge Luis Borges (Argentina, 1899–1986), the most toweringly influential figure in the shaping of modern Latin American literature.

The Urban and the Existential

The Argentine avant-garde centred on two groups, Florida and Boedo. In practice they were very similar, though the Boedo was thought to be more down to earth and connected with the popular classes. An influential member was Roberto Arlt (1900–42). Though virtually unknown outside of Latin America, Arlt would later become a cult figure among Boom authors such as Julio Cortázar. He is often re-membered for reorienting fiction away from the countryside towards more urban environments. His famous urban first novel, *El juguete rabioso* ('The Rabid Toy', 1926), came out in the same year as Güiraldes' rural elegy *Don Segundo Sombra*. Of course, what this really shows is that the 'modern' novel did not simply replace the 'traditional' one, but that the traditional and the modern existed side by side (often even within the same texts) and that the New Narrative emerged as part of a gradual and uneven process of change.

What is really significant about the urban turn in Arlt's fiction is what it represents: a break with the conventional social realism of regional fiction, and a new emphasis on ambiguity and existential as opposed to specifically social concerns. *El juguete rabioso* is not without its social realist dimension, but its original title, *La vida puerca* ('Life is Filthy'), alludes not just to the injustices of Buenos Aires society but to the very nature of human existence. The novel fixes relentlessly on dirt and degradation, and its protagonist Silvio Astier undergoes a series of humiliating trials until he feels 'tan pequeño frente a la vida, que yo no atinaba a coger una esperanza' ('so tiny in the face of life, that I couldn't come up with a single possibility of hope').[10] His attitude to sexuality underscores the inversion of traditional values; rather than a metaphor for fulfilment, the sexual act becomes a 'congojosa sequedad del espíritu, peregrina voluptuosidad áspera y mandadora' ('anguished drying-up of the spirit, a harsh and controlling wandering voluptuosity') (p. 52). There are expressions of optimism in the novel, but they seem to be constantly undone (the novel ends with Silvio engaging in an optimistic exchange, but then tripping over a chair). Like the character Erdosain, of whom Silvio is a forerunner and who botches his plan to murder someone in one of Arlt's later novels, Silvio engages in random and unsuccessful acts of villainy, such as arson. His setting fire to an aged tramp and his gratuitous betrayal of his friend Rengo are both signs of the absurdity of his life and his impotence in the face of it. Of course, Silvio is a rebel of sorts. But his independence of social and religious norms, coupled with his search for plenitude via self-degradation, basically mark him as a sort of absurd hero before the fact of existentialism.[11]

The centrality of the city and the break with the countryside as the crucible of identity are announced by the title of Argentine Leopoldo Marechal's (1900–70) 1948 novel *Adán Buenosayres* ('Adam Buenosaires'). But another Buenos Aires-set novel of the same year, *El túnel* ('The Tunnel') by Ernesto Sábato (1911–), brings out the sense of metaphysical malaise even more strongly. An accessible (and extremely readable) forerunner of the New Novel, it deals with a more upwardly mobile character than Silvio Astier, yet social difference does not seem to impact on existential condition. There is an obviously implied existential(ist) subtext in the novel's reference to Sartre and in the main character's sharing of his Christian names, Jean Paul. Despite the external reality setting of the anonymous big city, the accent is firmly on the individual and his subjective interior perception and construction of reality. Events are presented purely from the perspective of the deranged painter Juan Pablo Castel, whose obsessively possessive 'love' drives him to murder María Iribarne and leads to his subsequent incarceration in an asylum – the crime and the imprisonment obvious metaphors for the futile quest for communication and fulfilment.

Yet the point is that the novel establishes a link between psychology and the metaphysical. Castel's obsessive logic – which leads him to his misjudgements of María and his ultimate downfall – is a wider illustration of the limitations of reason, while his madness becomes a symbol of the chaos of the universe and the meaninglessness of human existence. The suggestion is that the madman is closer to the true nature of life and reality than the sane. This is the meaning of the image of the tunnel which gives the novel its title. Castel's sense of existential solitude is symbolized by the idea of living in a tunnel. He had hoped that the parallel tunnels in which he and María were living would one day converge, but he now recognizes that that can never be. What he realizes is that life is divided between those on either side of the tunnel's transparent walls: on the outside, the general populace who lead normal, everyday but shallow and dishonest lives; on the inside, those who, like Castel, have gained awareness of the fundamental absurdity of human life but who are therefore isolated from a world dependent on evasion for survival. Anticipating the centrality of the theme of solitude in much Latin American fiction, Castel says to María as he plunges his knife into her: 'Tengo que matarte, María. Me has dejado solo' ('I have to kill you, María. You've left me all alone').[12]

The main inheritor of the Arltian mantle was not really Sábato but the Uruguayan Juan Carlos Onetti (1909–94), a writer some critics regard as the essential link between the period after the avant-garde, the New Novel and the Boom. Onetti's short 1939 novel *El pozo* ('The Well' or, perhaps, 'The Pit') clearly uses internal reality in the presentation of the mind of protagonist Linacero. Equally importantly, it links the social to the metaphysical: the story of a social misfit in an alienating bourgeois environment soon becomes a tale of existential crisis following loss of faith in the meaningfulness of life. Fantasy (another key feature of future New Narrative) is an escape for Linacero, but only one that underlines the emptiness of reality. Linacero's story is in embryo that of Brausen, the hero of Onetti's 1950 novel *La vida breve* ('A Brief Life', 1950).

Donald Shaw, leading critic of the New Narrative, has made a convincing case for seeing *La vida breve* as the first novel of the Latin American Boom (see, e.g., Shaw 2002, pp. 110–12). Shaw notes three important features that establish a clear connection with the later, mature New Novel. The first is to do with the transition from reality to fantasy. Like Arlt's heroes, Brausen is a frustrated figure who seeks an outlet via self-degradation. He takes up an abusive relationship with a prostitute and, following her murder by an associate he has aided, flees Montevideo to take refuge in the town of Santa María. However, Santa María was previously nothing but an imaginary town to which Brausen escaped in his daydreams. The line between fiction and reality is comprehensively blurred, and such blurring would become a technical mainstay of later New Narrative. Moreover, Santa María would become the setting for most of Onetti's subsequent novels (which extended into the Boom and beyond), a model repeated in the famous fictional towns of, say, Comala (in Juan Rulfo's *Pedro Páramo*) and Macondo (in Gabriel García Márquez's *Cien años de soledad* ['One Hundred Years of Solitude']). The two other features noted by Shaw are the introduction of the figure of the author himself into the narrative and the self-referential allusions to the very act of the writing of the novel. Fiction, it seems, is no longer functioning as an unproblematic reflection of external reality. Fiction is now aware of the subjective nature of reality and of its own status as nothing but fiction.[13]

Jorge Luis Borges

Significantly, the title of what might be regarded as the most important, or at least most influential, book in the history of Latin American literature is *Ficciones* ('Fictions', 1944 and 1956). This is one of a number of collections of short stories by Argentina's Jorge Luis Borges. The example of Borges (that is, the example of his mature stories) is at the heart of the New Narrative. He is, in some ways, closer to Macedonio Fernández than to Sábato and Onetti, in the sense that his writing is characterized by scepticism rather than anguish. Metaphysics provides the main underpinning of his stories, but paradoxically is shown not to explain the nature of the universe but to prove its inexplicability.

Borges' favourite image is that of the labyrinth: an image of the universe itself, it suggests the appearance or possibility of order and the experience of disorientation and chaos. Typically, his stories deal with someone who is metaphorically seeking to make sense of the universe but who winds up lost in a labyrinth of incomprehension. An illustration of this view of the universe is 'La biblioteca de Babel' ('The Library of Babel'). Here the universe is presented as a vast library made up of an ever-repeating symmetrical chain of identical rooms containing books of identical format. The problem is the 'naturaleza informe y caótica de casi todos los libros' ('the formless and chaotic nature of nearly all the books'), that 'los libros nada significan en sí' ('the books mean nothing in themselves').[14] Generations of librarians have squandered their lives in trying to find meaning in the books, but all have failed. In other words, though, throughout time, the superficially ordered appearance of the universe has led human beings to seek to identify a hidden pattern or explanation, such a pattern or explanation has remained firmly beyond human grasp.

Belief systems for Borges are little more than the arbitrary inventions of human minds. So, when in 'La lotería en Babilonia' ('The Babylonian Lottery'), people choose to believe in an unseen company orchestrating the secret, free and universal lottery (an obvious image of the haphazard nature of life and the universe), this is an example of the human construction of religion as a means of explaining the inexplicable. But any human explanation is always limited and probably wrong. In 'Tlön, Uqbar, Orbis Tertius', humanity embraces the alternative world of Tlön because of its transparent orderliness. But Tlön is a non-existent place written about in a convincing-looking encyclopedia by a secret society: it is a world in a book, a fabrication of the human mind – it cannot explain a universe not created by man. Similarly, in the spy story 'El jardín de senderos que se bifurcan' ('The Garden of Forking Paths'), the mystery element of the spy genre is clarified at the end, but the tale of espionage frames an altogether less explicable story about a labyrinthine garden and book in which time seems to fork in different directions. Only the venal human mystery can be resolved: the greater enigma of time and life is beyond human reason.

One of Borges' favourite devices for showing up the limitations of human knowledge is the detective. In possibly his most famous story, 'La muerte y la brújula' ('Death and the Compass'), the sleuth Erik Lönnrot investigates the mysterious death of Dr Marcelo Yarmolinsky shortly before a Talmudic congress. Lönnrot believes the murder to be the work of a fanatical Hassidic sect and linked to the Tetragramatton, the secret name of God. One newspaper reports that 'el investigador Erik Lönnrot se había dedicado a estudiar los nombres de Dios para dar con el nombre del asesino' ('the detective Erik Lönnrot had dedicated himself to studying the names of God in order to come up with the name of the assassin') (p. 151). Lönnrot's quest, it is hinted, is symbolic of the human one to divine God's secret plan, that is to find the key to the mystery of the universe. The point is that Lönnrot gets it wrong: his Holmesian deductive logic leads him to precisely the incorrect conclusion. Yarmolinsky's murder seems to be part of a series, but the first crime was simply a mistake (they got the wrong man); after hearing that Lönnrot was assuming a motive based in Jewish mysticism, his arch enemy Red Scharlach planted an elaborate series of clues to trap Lönnrot. Thus when Lönnrot sets out to catch his killer at the end, it transpires that he is himself the last intended victim and the story concludes with his death. Reason is thoroughly undone here. Indeed when Lönnrot enters near the end the bewilderingly labyrinthine mansion where Scharlach is lying in wait, Lönnrot's disillusionment represents the undermining of all human theories of the key to life. Moreover, he and Scharlach talk as if this contest between them has taken place before and will again in the future: throughout time, humanity has been and will be compelled to repeat the same quest and experience the same failure.

The above can give the merest impression of the textured intricacy of Borges' stories. Essentially, his tales are complex puzzles in which the reader is lured into the game of decipherment only to end up as confused as the characters. In Borges, the reader has to play an active role, but his or her logical engagement yields no ultimate truths. The reader has a radically different experience to the passive security of a realist text. She or he is reminded of the limited nature of the intellect, the irreducible nature of reality, and fiction's inability to establish a transparent, one-to-one relationship with external reality. Indeed reality itself is akin to a fiction, in that it is always in some ways a construction of the human mind. Some would argue that this leads to pessimism in Borges. However, there is little emotion in these very cerebral stories. His position is more that of the amused sceptic, recognizing that human beings (himself included) will inevitably be continually drawn to speculations on the meaning of life even though they can never know if they have the right answer. In this sense, his stories are very much like games, because that is what thought, philosophy, theory and art are: the game of creating convincing versions or explanations of life that can never be proven. It is perhaps this game-playing which was Borges' major gift to Latin American letters. It is probably a mistake to see Borges himself as advancing philosophy in any major way. What he did was to free the mind, to assert fully literature's freedom from its immediate context or external reality. He helped to free fiction to be about whatever it wanted to be about. It was this sense of freedom from conventional literary constraints which was to give the Latin American New Narrative its unique character.[15]

Of course, Borges has his detractors. Indeed he has been severely attacked for his political disengagement and inauguration of a literary tradition fundamentally unconnected to Latin American social reality. It is not entirely true that Borges' stories are divorced from the Latin American context. Many, most famously 'El Sur' ('The South'), deal with the intellectual's complex relationship with Argentine national tradition and update the whole Civilization and Barbarism debate.[16] And, more recently, critics have begun to reassess Borges through a more obviously historical-political lens.[17] None the less, new historical re-examinations will not change the fact that Borges' key influence was at the level of literariness and questions about fiction, reality and the relationships between the two. But the very fact that even this most un-American of (South) Americans does have a real social and political dimension to his work should remind us that the New Narrative does not mean the abandonment of socio-political concerns or of the Latin American experience. Just as avant-garde tendencies developed hand in hand with the growth of Regionalism, so too was there an important, evolving strand of anti-traditional experimental writing that was very much involved with the issue of defining Latin American identity. This was the strand that would ultimately give the world, for better or worse, the popular notion of Magical Realism.

Magical Realism

Magical Realism[18] bridges the gap between social realist regional fiction and fantasy or formal innovation. It demonstrates an understanding of the difference between perception and reality, and it involves the assimilation of European technical virtuosity in order to explore better the character of a specifically Latin American reality. In its essence, Magical Realism is based on the belief that Latin America is somehow unusual or 'marvellous' because of its extraordinary extremes of history, geography, development, religion and ethnicity – that its reality is actually quite close to fantasy. This would lead eventually to a style of narrative (associated most commonly with Gabriel García Márquez; see chapter 4) whose particular effect lay in the way in which bizarre events were described naturally (the basic hallmark of the genre, if it can be termed as such).

Magical Realism, in its modern Latin American sense, really begins with the Cuban Alejo Carpentier (1904–80), whose literary career stretches from the European avant-garde through to the Boom and after.[19] Throughout the 1930s he came into close contact with the French Surrealists in Paris. Upon his return home at the end of the decade and following a highly formative trip to Haiti in 1943, he began to see the European idea of the surreal as part of everyday life in his own land. His early Afro-Cuban novel *¡Ecue-Yamba O!* (1933), for instance, favourably opposes black primitivism to white dominance. More interesting is *El reino de este mundo* ('The Kingdom of this World') of 1949, in whose famous prologue he coined the phrase *lo real maravilloso* or the 'marvellous real'. The novel deals with familiar Latin American themes of independence, progress and national and cultural legitimization in its account of Haiti's transition in the late eighteenth and early nineteenth centuries from slave revolts to black rule. What makes the novel different is the way it presents external reality from the perspective of a former slave steeped in ancient oral tradition and magical beliefs. This is the effect of the 'marvellous real' – history and reality are transformed as the reader is allowed to see them from the magical perspective of Ti Noel.

The problem is that the technique does not really work. The point of view is somewhere uncomfortably in between the modern and the traditional, the black and the white, the European and the Caribbean. In a sense, *lo real maravilloso* is a fatally flawed concept in that it implicitly invites an implied Latin American reader to gawp at his or her own Latin American reality as if it were a marvel. It unwittingly reasserts an outsider's European-tinged view of Latin American identity at the very moment that it tries to authenticate a genuinely third world vision. Carpentier's problem is brought out vividly by one of his own protagonists, the narrator of his 1953 novel *Los pasos perdidos* ('The Lost Steps'). Here a US-based and European-influenced musician of mixed European and Latin American parentage has the opportunity to journey deep into a remote region of Latin America in order to unearth primitive musical instruments. The materialist and pretentious North and the West are unnatural and alienating, while the odyssey into the southern jungle is portrayed as a journey back in time towards primitivism and authenticity. Though there is much positive valorization of the simpler, more meaningful jungle culture, the fact remains that the narrator cannot settle or fit in and finally needs to return north. The title comes from his subsequent failed attempt to retrace his steps back. The European or general Western cultural influence and pull are so great that the Latin American intellectual will always remain alien to the realities of his own subcontinent, no matter how nobly he tries to recuperate a sense of originary identity.

Neo-Indigenism

An integral feature of what is now called Magical Realism is the indigenous population's view of life, based on myth and legend. Thus an important related phenomenon in the first half of the twentieth century was the revival of Indigenism. Indigenist writing, however well intentioned in its honest desire to bring the plight of the Indians to wider attention, often offered an outsider's view from a clearly outside position (see chapters 1 and 2). What some have come to call Neo-Indigenism or *neoindigenismo* attempted to recreate the indigenous experience from the inside, that is to show reality through the filter of the indigenous population's perception of it. Of course, many of these experiments pre-date any comprehensive notion of Neo-Indigenism or Magical Realism.

In Brazil, for instance, Mário de Andrade's (1893–1945) *Macunaíma* (1928), written in the wake of the Semana de Arte Moderna, was a São Paulo intellectual's effort at melding avant-garde *modernismo* with an empathy for primitivism in order to produce a mythical narrative of cultural roots. Macunaíma is a mythical, magical, Amazonian tribal figure whom Mário turns into a kind of metaphor for Brazil. The thinking behind this discursive strategy comes from Oswald de Andrade's (1890–1954) famous 'Manifesto antropófago' ('Cannibalistic Manifesto', 1928), which inverted Civilization and Barbarism by advocating a kind of return to the early Indian practice of absorbing the European enemy's strength by eating them; only now it is writers and artists who must break the ultimate taboo by ingesting, as it were, European influences in order to generate an authentically Brazilian culture. In Mário's novel, Macunaíma represents this pulsating possibility of authentic multiracial multiculturalism, but his death after a self-tainting trip to the big city shows the danger of sacrificing authenticity to foreign notions of progress.

Though clearly an early forerunner of Magical Realism, the novel is only Neo-Indigenist in the way it seeks to imagine a magical Indian world view on its own terms. But, of course, in the case of Brazil, Mário is not referring to any real or specific Indian group. That is more the territory of another important foundational figure in Magical Realism and Neo-Indigenism, the Guatemalan Miguel Angel Asturias (1899–1974). Asturias, an ethnologist by training, was in Paris with Carpentier and undertook a similar project, to use the Surrealist fascination with the unconscious in order to create a seemingly authentic Indian voice that would express native experience. His first offering, *Leyendas de Guatemala* ('Legends of Guatemala', 1930), a literary-anthropological replaying of folk tales and myths, very much eschews any notion of the anthropologist's distance from the subject and reformulates the legends with great sensitivity. His 1949 novel *Hombres de maíz* ('Men of Maize') goes further, seemingly mimicking the syntax of indigenous speech and following a mythical rather than plot-based structure. Moreover, phenomena such as form-shifting from human to animal are presented totally naturally. Though the novel is about the corruption of a natural relationship with the land via the thirst for profit, the Indians are presented not as helpless victims (a criticism that has been levelled at traditional Indigenist novels), but as a people who adapt skilfully in ways that allow them to retain their culture as well as affect positively the culture of others.

Asturias' most famous novel was not specifically about Indians and will be considered presently. First, though, we must turn to the author probably most closely associated with the idea of Neo-Indigenism in Latin America, Peru's José María Arguedas (1911–69). A rather different figure to Asturias, he had limited contact with Europe and his first language was actually the indigenous Andean Quechua. His best novel is *Los ríos profundos* ('Deep Rivers', 1958). The semi-autobiographical narrator of the novel is the young white boy Ernesto, who, having partly grown up in a rural Indian community or *ayllu*, is made, as an adolescent, to enter a religious boarding school in the town of Abancay. Confusion and alienation ensue as his meaningful and harmonious Indian upbringing is contradicted by the division, cruelty and repression of the white school. Much of the novel is given over to bringing out this contrast. The school is a literal stand-in for white society and the oligarchical alliance of church, state and land, in that the corrupt priests unquestioningly support the mean-spirited landowners and use religion to hold the Indians back. On a more metaphorical level the school's culture of rivalry, violence, bullying and sexual abuse represents the more general decadence of so-called 'civilized' society. But (in yet another inversion of the traditional civilization-versus-barbarism dichotomy) against the degraded white world stands the magical world of meaningful indigenous tradition into which Ernesto tries to escape. He frequents the local bars or *chicherías*, where he listens to *huaynos*, Quechua songs. He immerses his mind in the contemplation of the natural scenery of the surrounding countryside. And he pursues the ideal of the *zumbayllu*, a sort of supernatural spinning-top which he believes will attract the harmony of the natural world into the hostile environment of the school.

What is really significant about all this with regard to the development of the novel is the method of presentation. Events are recorded very much from the child-cum-indigenous perspective. There is no conventionally rational distinction made here between human being and nature, or between external reality and spiritual or supernatural belief. The viewpoint is a mystical-mythic one based on the indigenous synthesis of man and nature as an integrated whole. Moreover, though this is clearly not a break with social protest, it is a step forward from the perceived easy didacticism and external observation of earlier Indigenist works. Two key political episodes in the novel are the revolt of the *chicheras* or female bar workers protesting against the rationing of salt, and the rebellion of the *colonos* (basically serf-like indigenous peasants tied to the large *haciendas* or estates) provoked by the outbreak of a plague. Yet Ernesto lacks the ideological framework to see these in explicitly political terms and so understands them on a magical-spiritual level: the leader of the *chicheras*, Doña Felipa, becomes a mythical figure linked to the river, the sun and the *zumbayllu*, invulnerable to danger; the Indians are seen to march as one to scare off the 'fever', which is conceived of as a supernatural evil spirit.

The question is whether this type of technical presentation sharpens or dilutes the political impact, a dilemma which would not go (and still has not gone) away for writers who sought to reconcile social protest with a somewhat contrary trend towards subjectivity and ambiguity. Can the *colonos'* 'supernatural' victory presage material change in 'real' terms? Is their uprising (which is basically to demand a special mass to ward off disease) little more than a disguised manifestation of subservience to white authority? Do their traditional beliefs, even if in some ways morally superior to those of white culture, act as a barrier to practical social and economic progress? The novel does not really answer such questions. The way out of this interpretative bind is to see the ambiguity as itself politically meaningful. Ernesto is fundamentally in between cultures. The implication is that the positive way forward is transculturation, that is a mutually enriching cultural interchange in a reformed Peru which values and builds from its cultural diversity.[20]

Two Great New Novels

What has been emerging from this analysis of the rise of the New Narrative is that it is not a simple matter of the modern displacing the traditional, but a rather more subtle and elusive process. Essentially, two broad trends can be identified. First, the crisis of modernity leads to the disintegration of long-standing belief systems, and this malaise is brought out by narrative forms that reflect uncertainty or even chaos. Second, modernity offers exhilarating new ways of reading the world that can be adapted in narrative to create a more authentic expression of Latin American identity. In practice, both positions have their limitations and contradictions, and they interact with each other in ways that are complex and sometimes difficult to fathom. For example, the rejection of modernity is usually enunciated via the very narrative techniques of modernism, while at the same time the embracing of modernist methods to affirm cultural identity often involves a rejection of the wider values associated with modernity.

These differences cannot be effectively resolved and have provoked various and often bitter debates (see chapter 7). At this stage, the main point to make about the rise of the New Novel at the dawn of the Boom is that the New Narrative is inescapably characterized by a tension between Europe and Latin America, North and South, the universal and the specific, the existential and the political. Perhaps it is in the very ambiguity of this position that much of the literary appeal of the New Narrative lies. So, to conclude this chapter, we will examine two of the most remarkable examples of the New Novel from before the Boom of the 1960s, novels which bring out the aforementioned tensions but which also have an unprecedented renovatory effect as literature: *El Señor Presidente* (1946, though written roughly between 1922 and 1932) by the 1967 Nobel Prize winner from Guatemala, Miguel Angel Asturias, and *Pedro Páramo* (1955) by Mexico's Juan Rulfo (1918–86).

El Señor Presidente

The opening of *El Señor Presidente* (tr. 'The President') has been de-scribed as the first pages of the New Novel.[21] A major novel of dicta-torship, it is based on the regime of Manuel Estrada Cabrera, who ruled Guatemala with an iron fist from 1898 to 1920. However, the president of the title is never named, nor is the country, nor is the time. The novel is set, then, in no particular time or place. This was a radical break with other narratives, which had been traditionally judged according to how well they reflected reality. Now the novel was to be judged as an autonomous reality in its own right, that is as a work of fiction. This is what sets *El Señor Presidente* apart and makes it such an important forerunner of the New Novel: although it seems to deal with Latin American specificity and does, it has to be said, have many realist moments, it effectively dares to announce itself as, above all else, a work of fiction.

Indeed the novel has virtually none of the traditional apparatus of mainstream prose narrative. For instance, there is no real plot to speak of and no convincing or consistent characters. Instead the text employs alternative devices such as a mythical substructure or the repetition of motifs: a sketchy framework makes the text viable as narrative, but leaves the writer free to introduce whatever elements he likes, while giving the reader a more active and reconstructive role. A simple example should suffice. At one stage, two of the principal characters stumble across a drunken and incomprehensible mailman, dropping and losing his letters as he goes. The episode contributes nothing to the plot, but is typical of a repeated series of scenes indicating failure of communication. The reader reads the text as an indictment of the breakdown of meaningful social networks under dictatorship, but through associative inference rather than thanks to explicit narratorial guidance.

In a sense, expression is beginning to take precedence over elucidation. And one of the most striking features of the novel is its expressive use of language. Language is often broken up to give a sense of the frayed nerves of individuals living under a dictatorship or, more commonly, to imply the distorted values that hold sway in the regime. For example: the lottery ticket vendor Tío Fulgencio's garbled Spanish is itself an illustration of the meaninglessly haphazard and lottery-like value system of the president's regime; Mrs Carvajal's hysterical stuttering of the nonsensical phrase '¡le, le, le!' ('la, la, la!') is a sign of the shattering of her faith in justice (it is probably a fragment of the once meaningful word 'ley' or 'law', now turned into a travesty by the *auditor* or judge advocate who confirms her husband's arbitrary but imminent summary execution, 'conforme a la ley' ['in accordance with the law']).[22] The characters, meantime, are themselves presented expressionistically as esperpentic[23] caricatures. Many have absurd and sometimes animal nicknames. The beggars are crazy and wildly deformed, and the scene where they are tortured has a zany, slapstick wackiness about it. The gigantic Doña Venjamón holds up and dangles her diminutive puppeteer husband Don Benjamín so that he himself looks like a like a puppet from one of his own shows. The characters are effectively dehumanized and reduced to mere puppets in the alienating context of dictatorship – hence the sometimes unremarked sourly comic element, which reinforces the loss of dignity.

More generally, the expressionism of myth projects the president as an omnipotent and omnipresent force, a mix of Christian and Mayan deities. The equation of the Indian god Tohil, greedy for human sacrifice, with the Christian God suggests an inversion of traditional Western beliefs based on Christianity. Here the God is evil, reigning over an infernal world where all values have been turned upside down. The inverted myth is continued in the identification of the novel's principal character, Miguel Cara de Angel, with the fallen angel Lucifer. Cara de Angel falls from the president's favour when he falls for the daughter of one of the president's enemies. But now the rebellious angel is rebelling against evil in the name of love. The power of love seems to be an important theme in the novel. When Camila, the object of Cara de Angel's affection, is forcibly separated from her father and caring nanny, she literally begins to die. Cara de Angel now accelerates his transition from presidential henchman to decent human being in the hope that acts of kindness and love will be repaid by Camila's survival. Eventually she is saved by marriage, on the advice of a character called Tícher (a pun on Teacher), who counsels: 'a la muerte únicamente se le puede oponer el amor' ('the only thing that can oppose death is love') (p. 212). And although the couple are eventually torn apart and Cara de Angel dies a forlorn death in the deepest, darkest dungeon, there are possible hints of regeneration and perhaps even salvation in the birth of their son.

What is perhaps most notable about the story of Cara de Angel and Camila is not just its ultimate ambiguity, but that their rebellion takes absolute precedence over the other rebellion in the novel – the political one of General Canales to be launched against the corrupt regime. This is the only example of constructive collective activity in the novel, yet little is told about it and it fizzles out almost as soon as it starts.

The suggestion seems to be that political change is not just a matter of swapping one system for another, but must come at the most elemental level with human beings learning mutual respect and love. This humanization of struggle certainly creates a richer literary experience. The question is what this vague programme of respect and love might mean in concrete political terms. It seems that the political level risks being fudged by the presentational ambiguities. It is difficult to comment effectively on political reality if the very vehicle of that comment appears to undermine its own application to reality.[24]

Pedro Páramo

A similar problem emerges with regard to *Pedro Páramo*. This novel can be – indeed has been and continues to be – read as another version of the novel of the Mexican Revolution (see chapter 2). It is a critique of *caciquismo*, that is of the power of corrupt landowners, and, at the same time, of the Revolution against such corruption, whose principles are seen to be betrayed. Yet the *cacique*, in this case the Pedro Páramo of the title, is presented internally as well as externally, placed in a psychological context that helps explain his actions, and even presented as a victim himself – of an oppressive upbringing and unrequited love. Moreover, the Revolution is clearly of little or no interest to the inhabitants of Comala (the town where the novel is set), who are only vaguely aware of some sort of trouble in the hills, and, most crucially, of virtually no concern to the *cacique*, supposedly one of the main targets of the Revolution (on a number of occasions when he is given important information on the progress of the struggle, his mind wanders instead to thoughts of the woman he has loved and lost, Susana San Juan). If this is not enough, most of the novel is not really about the *cacique* at all, but about a young man's failed search for his father, a woman's obsession with her dead lover, the frustrations of a failed and sinful priest, and a whole series of other stories of lost illusions. To cap it all, all of the characters in the novel turn out to be dead, chattering about their pasts in their grave or with their spirits wandering the land. And, finally, the narrative form is so bafflingly fragmented that it is quite clear that this novel is a very long way indeed from the traditional novel of protest.

Although critics still read *Pedro Páramo* as a specifically Mexican take on life and as an implied attack on aspects of Mexican society, and although they often rage against universalist readings of Latin American literature, it seems naive to the point of absurdity to deny that there is an overwhelmingly existential dimension to this work. We may or may not choose to see the landowner as an inverted God figure, like Asturias' president.[25] However, we cannot fail to notice the general theme of loss of faith and the crushing of dreams. The first story is that of how young Juan Preciado comes to Comala, a land described to him in idyllic terms by his recently deceased mother, to seek out his long-lost father, one Pedro Páramo. But Comala is a ghost town and his father is dead. Although Juan's motivation for his journey is that 'comencé a llenarme de sueños, a darle vuelo a las ilusiones', 'y de este modo se me fue formando un mundo alrededor de la esperanza' ('I began to fill myself up with dreams, to give flight to my illusions', 'and in this way there began to form in my mind a world full of hope'), he quickly comes to the conclusion that his search has led him to the opposite: 'A un pueblo solitario. Buscando a alguien que no existe' ('To a solitary village. Looking for someone who does not exist').[26]

The stories of all the other characters follow this same pattern of illusion giving way to despair, supported by the imagery of the fall from grace. At one stage, Juan meets a fallen couple, living in incest. They are naked (as God made them, it is commented) and are said to have been there forever. When a bishop refused to forgive their sin, his words of punishment echoed those of God to Adam and Eve in the Garden of Eden. The woman is now tormented by her sin and feels that her guilt must show like the stain of original sin. Unable to gain entry to paradise, their tormented souls must roam in grief forever. This condition turns out be that of the whole of Comala (ostensibly because the sinful parish priest could not grant absolution and the whole community has died outside a state of grace). The glimpse of paradise overtaken by the reality of the fall is a basic principle of the narrative. And so, when Juan is seduced by the incestuous sister, this possible moment of fulfilment is really a loss of innocence: she disintegrates into a pile of slime and Juan dies shortly after, probably of fright. '¿La ilusión?', comments one of his graveyard companions, 'Eso cuesta caro' ('Illusions? You pay a high price for those') (p. 64).

A striking feature is that after the shock of the incestuous sister's physical disintegration, chronological time disintegrates too, 'como si se hubiera retrocedido el tiempo' ('as if time had started to go back-wards') (p. 58). This breakdown in Juan Preciado's sense of time echoes the structure of the novel as a whole, which constantly zigzags backwards and forwards in time and place. Time is, of course, in many ways, a human invention and a means of imposing an artificial order on the flux of experience. In challenging our notion of time, the novel is challenging the very means we use to make sense of life. If the novel is fundamentally about loss of faith, then the fragmentary narrative structure reinforces the sensation of disorientation, confusion and anxiety that such a crisis of belief brings. The reader is thus made – through form as much as content – to share the unease and loss of certainty that is the lot of the characters and, possibly, it is suggested, humanity. He or she is made to struggle with the narrative puzzle in the same way as with life, without the benefit of any clear answers or solutions at the end. At the very least, the reader is made to wake up to the profoundly ambiguous nature of reality. On a literary level, then, the great leap forward represented by a novel like *Pedro Páramo* is the dramatic change it effects in the role of the reader, from passive recipient to active agent. This would also be the great achievement of the Boom.

CHAPTER 4

The Boom

The chronology of the Latin American Boom is as straightforward or as complex as literary critics want to make it. The most useful way to understand it is as the climax of the New Narrative, the sort of experimental fiction that appeared to break self-consciously with imagined traditional realist models and posit a more problematic vision of reality and literature's relation to it. The New Narrative, though its roots can be traced further back, became significant in the 1940s and 1950s, but achieved canonical status and international projection in the 1960s with the Boom. The Boom is, in many ways, a phenomenon of publishing, consumption and reception. It marks the period when Latin American, or more particularly Spanish American, fiction became internationally visible on some scale for the first time.

A number of factors aided this process of internationalization. One was the Cuban Revolution of 1959, which put Latin America on the world map, promoted new interest in the region and made its cultural output marketable as one of alternative perspectives, and helped foster a sense of cross-national subcontinental identity, identification and community amongst different Spanish American authors. A more or less simultaneous phenomenon was the massive promotion of Spanish American writing in Spain.[1]

Literary production in Spain had been pretty moribund in the post-Civil War period of the Franco dictatorship, apart from some rather earnest social realist fiction, and was further hampered by official state censorship. Not only was the Spanish American New Narrative more exciting as literature, it could also stand in, in terms of content and attitude, for domestically prohibited revolutionary criticism of an oppressive militaristic state. Two key figures in Spain were the Spanish publisher Carlos Barral and the Spanish literary agent Carmen Balcells. Many practitioners of the Spanish American New Novel were, for various reasons, living in Spain or elsewhere in Europe, and Balcells was instrumental in transforming them into professional writers. Moreover, Barral was one of a group of ambitious publishers keen to promote international writing via schemes such as highly visible annual gatherings of writers, critics and publishers and the award of literary prizes. One such prize was the Biblioteca Breve Prize of the Barcelona-based Seix Barral publishing house, a prize which – in many minds – became intimately associated with the fortunes of the Spanish American New Novel.

As the New Novel was becoming established in Europe, a further development helped consolidate its status. This was the founding in Paris in 1966 of the highly influential literary magazine *Mundo Nuevo* ('New World'), which became a kind of flagship for the New Narrative as well as a debating point for issues of Latin American cultural interest. Though it was attacked from the left (especially in Cuba), has been accused of Eurocentrism, and was even demonstrated to have been effectively funded and supported by the CIA, the journal did play a very significant role in raising consciousness about Latin American writing for a brief but important period in the mid-to-late sixties. Its founder, the Uruguayan critic Emir Rodríguez Monegal, was himself a tireless promoter of Spanish American narrative. He became a noted professor in the USA, and the rise of Latin Americanism as an academic discipline in the US, supported by invitations to Latin American writers to speak or enjoy short tenures there, was another factor in the cementing of the reputation of the New Novel.

So, when does the Boom begin and end? One simple way of dating it is via the Biblioteca Breve Prize. The award of the prize in 1962 to the young Peruvian Mario Vargas Llosa (1936–) for his astounding novel *La ciudad y los perros* (tr. 'The Time of the Hero', formally published 1963) – the first time a non-Spaniard had ever won the prize – is often seen as the beginning of the Boom. Carlos Barral's split from Seix Barral and the suspension of the prize in 1970 is sometimes seen as the end of the Boom: the novel which would have won it that year, *El obsceno pájaro de la noche* ('The Obscene Bird of Night') by Chile's José Donoso (1924–96) has been seen as the phenomenon's endpoint, after which a Post-Boom can be seen to emerge (see chapter 5). However, there are all sorts of rival claims. Others date the start of the Boom as 1958 with the publication of the first major work (*La región más transparente* [tr. 'Where the Air is Clear']) by one of the gurus of the New Narrative, Mexico's Carlos Fuentes (1928–). Some see the confinement of the Boom to the 1960s as limited, and argue that it really began in 1950 with Juan Carlos Onetti's *La vida breve* or even (though this is stretching it) with Miguel Angel Asturias' *El Señor Presidente* (1946).[2] Many would note too that what must be regarded as major examples of the New Narrative appeared after 1970, such as Gabriel García Márquez's (Colombia, 1928–) *El otoño del patriarca* ('The Autumn of the Patriarch', 1975), Augusto Roa Bastos' (Paraguay, 1918–) *Yo el Supremo* ('I the Supreme', 1974), or Fuentes' *Terra Nostra* (1975).

This dating game also raises questions about who should be included in the Boom. Is Juan Rulfo precursor or protagonist? What about Alejo Carpentier and Onetti, who also wrote major novels in the 1960s and 1970s? And are writers like Guillermo Cabrera Infante (Cuba, 1929–) and Manuel Puig (Argentina, 1932–90), who wrote important novels in the late sixties, products of the Boom or can they be more fruitfully associated with the idea of the Post-Boom? Then there is the question of Brazil. Some would say that Brazil does not really form part of the Boom at all, and note that there was little comparable fiction of quality produced there in the 1960s, while others would cite João Guimarães Rosa (1908–67) or Clarice Lispector (1920–77) as possible candidates for inclusion. The arguments could be endless.[3] The question of a possible Post-Boom will be considered in the next chapter, but by and large the Boom is a phenomenon of the 1960s and of Spanish America. A number of big novels by established writers appeared in this period, as well as significant ones by new figures. But the Boom is concentrated around four central figures, the so-called Big Four: Fuentes, Vargas Llosa, García Márquez and Argentina's Julio Cortázar (1914–84).

The Big Four

Julio Cortázar

Cortázar's *Rayuela* ('Hopscotch', 1963) is in many ways the quintessential novel of the Boom and of the 1960s. It typified the sort of experimentation associated with the New Novel. The book consists of fifty-six chapters, but then there are a further ninety-nine extra chapters which the reader can add in to form a second book. What is more, the author provides a chart at the beginning of the novel to suggest an alternative way of reading the text that challenges the idea of a traditional chronological sequence. Obviously, the conventional assumption of literature as a mirror of reality is being exploded here, with reality being presented as an ambiguous and complex phenomenon that is negotiated subjectively. An important figure in the so-called dispensable extra chapters is that of Morelli (based partly, it seems, on Macedonio Fernández [see chapter 3]) who offers a series of reflections on the processes of writing and reading. Morelli seems to critique an imagined realist novel that presents the reader with a recognizably enclosed but therefore fundamentally limited world. He calls the traditional reader of such texts a *lector-hembra*, a kind of 'feminine' (in a pre-feminist sense) or passive reader who simply accepts what he or she is told. He argues instead for a type of writing that will appeal to a *lector-cómplice*, a reader as accomplice, who will play a much more active and constructive role in the narrative. *Rayuela* itself becomes, then, an aspirational version of Morelli's ideal novel in which the reader recreates his or her own text as he or she leaves the passive comfort of the armchair to jump about creatively, as in a game of hopscotch, in order to build his or her own narrative experience.

Cortázar's novel is self-consciously playful and artificial, constantly drawing attention to its own literariness and strategies of construction. It contains all sorts of absurdities and non sequiturs, and dwells too on the deceptive nature of language itself, which has deluded people into false beliefs about the nature of human experience. Yet the hopscotch narrative form does also suggest some sort of endgame. As many critics have noted,[4] the novel is driven by the idea of a quest. Cortázar seems to have been influenced by the Surrealist idea of a possible state of plenitude stemming from the fusion of the conscious and the unconscious, and literature comes across as a means to achieve a new level of insight, called – variously and amongst other things – a centre, yonder or kibbutz of desire. The working title for *Rayuela* was *Mandala*, and the Buddhist concept of the mandala as a kind of labyrinth through which humans progress towards a centre or revelation seems to inform its construction. Yet the notion is vague and paradoxical. In destroying language one can arrive at a new, intuitive form of understanding, yet – as author and reader – one remains tied to the very language one seeks to deconstruct. This obscure and never clearly resolved metaphysical quest lies at the heart of the novel's plot, such as it is.

Apart from the supposedly expendable extra chapters, the novel is divided between what is called 'Del lado de allá' (the far side of Paris) and 'Del lado de acá' (the near side of Buenos Aires), suggesting the hope of the reconciliation of divisions and the attainment of a state of fusion. The frustrated Argentine Horacio Oliveira hangs out in Paris, fairly aimlessly for the most part. He finds a Uruguayan girlfriend, la Maga, and spends much of his time in long-winded conversations on intellectual matters and the arts with his friends from the so-called Club de la Serpiente or Serpent Club. During one of these discussions, he leaves Maga to find her child, Rocamadour, dead in another room, after which he goes down to join a bunch of tramps in a place beneath a bridge and is arrested, drunk, while one of them is sucking his penis. Unable to find Maga, he ends up back in Buenos Aires, working in a circus and a lunatic asylum, until he betrays his friend Traveler by kissing his wife Talita. Talita is confused in his mind with Maga, and his story (and life?) ends with him seeming to leap to her from a windowsill (she is standing on a hopscotch pattern below).

This apparent aimlessness, however, hides a deeper search. The novel begins with the question: '¿Encontraría a la Maga?' ('Would I ever find Maga?')[5] The search for the uncultured Maga represents the possible fusion of intellect and intuition, reason and instinct, mind and body. And Oliveira's journey is not dissimilar to the Arltian or Onettian quest for fulfilment through self-degradation. So, the leap into the hopscotch pattern at the end of his story may be a leap into the void or into a new dimension – existential oblivion or the acquisition of authenticity.

Cortázar's fiction does often seem to display a belief in the possibility of reaching this ill-defined goal of insight, making the transition, as he sometimes calls it, from *el hombre viejo* ('the old self') to *el hombre nuevo* ('the new self') – even if the quest always seems to fail. This can be seen most easily in his splendid short stories, such as those of *Todos los fuegos el fuego* ('All the Fires the Fire', 1966). In 'La isla a mediodía' ('The Island at Midday'), for example, the air-steward Marini abandons (albeit probably via fantasy) his empty, humdrum lifestyle (symbolized by the routine of his air schedule) to go back to nature in the paradisaical Greek island over which his aeroplane flies every day. However, he is unable to tear himself away from the sight of the plane and, when it crashes into the sea, cannot prevent himself from swimming towards it. Symbolically, of course, he is rejoining his old self. The fact that the only thing new on the island at the end of the story is Marini's washed-up corpse underlines the failure of his enterprise. Yet, while on the island, Marini felt that 'no sería fácil matar al hombre viejo, pero allí en lo alto, tenso de sol y de espacio, sintió que la empresa era posible' ('it would not be easy to kill off the old self, but high up there, in a place tense with sun and space, he felt that such an undertaking was possible').[6] But this is not what happens elsewhere.

In one of Cortázar's best stories, 'El otro cielo' ('The Other Sky'), a young man flits fantastically from the dreary, oppressive world of Buenos Aires in the 1940s to the more fascinating underworld of pimps, prostitutes and macabre murder that are seen to characterize parts of Paris in the 1860s. Here he becomes intrigued by a bohemian writer known only as the 'sudamericano' or South American (a complex echo of the French author of South American origin Lautréamont, nicknamed the Montevidean, whose works give the story its epigraphs, and the tale's instinctive strangler Laurent). The 'sudamericano' in some ways represents the potential transition from the rational Buenos Aires self to the imaginative Parisian self. But, in a crucial scene, the young narrator is unable to act upon his urge to make contact with him:

> no me acuerdo bien de lo que sentía al renunciar a mi impulso, pero era algo como una veda, el sentimiento de que si la trasgredía iba a entrar en un territorio inseguro. Y sin embargo creo que hice mal, que estuve al borde de un acto que hubiera podido salvarme. (p. 146)

> (I don't remember very well what I felt when I renounced my impulse, but it was something like a taboo, the feeling that if I transgressed it I would enter into a more insecure territory. And, nevertheless, I think I did the wrong thing, that I was on the edge of an act that could have saved me.)

The transition to an ideal state is ultimately impossible to make. Perhaps a more practical possibility for the 'hombre nuevo', then, is political revolution. In the (revealingly rather poor) story 'Reunión', the idea of the 'new self' is linked to Fidel Castro and Che Guevara.

Indeed, Cortázar's literary and public life became increasingly identified with the political left as his career developed. His 1973 novel *Libro de Manuel* (tr. 'A Manual for Manuel') seeks a reconciliation between existential and political ideals. It deals with a group of political activists-cum-guerrillas, but bizarrely presents a character's act of sodomizing his bourgeois lover as a key moment of liberation. Cortázar's desire to raise literary transgression to the heights of political revolution was never really entirely successful. The essential fuzziness of his transgressive programme is its obvious limitation, as is its tendency to undermine itself by a sense of existential failure. Perhaps Cortázar's really important influence was at the mainly literary level. Though many of his stories stand the test of time, his principal novel, *Rayuela*, now seems trapped in a semi-hippy, jazz-fuelled, sixties time warp. Its main import was probably that it managed to encapsulate the literary aesthetic of the Boom: a sense of a radical break with a perceived tradition and a desire to jolt the reader out of complacency and into a more active engagement with a much more ambiguous notion of both literature and reality.

Carlos Fuentes

If *Rayuela* was a kind of model of the New Narrative, then the New Novel's main cultural ambassador was probably Carlos Fuentes. Still writing and still very much the roving commentator popping up all over the place in the press and on television, Fuentes is often mentioned as one of the great promoters of Latin American literature, and his 1969 book *La nueva novela hispanoamericana* ('The Latin American New Novel') was a central articulation of the ethos of the New Narrative by one of its own practitioners. His main contention was that the New Novel's achievement was to free itself from the simplicity and descriptiveness of previous writing in the region, and his own *La región más transparente* is quoted by many novelists as an influential and emblematic manifestation of this liberating aesthetic. However, while Fuentes is a towering intellectual presence, it is doubtful that he can be considered a great novelist like, say, García Márquez or Vargas Llosa (though, of course, not all would agree).

Fuentes' best, or at least most often praised, novel is probably *La muerte de Artemio Cruz* ('The Death of Artemio Cruz') from 1962, but he has no single great novel to compare with *Rayuela* or García

Márquez's *Cien años de soledad,* and his reputation depends more on his continued and prolific output as a whole. One can see why *La región más transparente* was influential. Reminiscent of North America's John Dos Passos, it offers a fragmentary and kaleidoscopic vision of modern Mexican society with a technical panache that now seems contrived. Still, it is an important forerunner of what Vargas Llosa would later call *la novela totalizadora* or 'totalizing novel' in its dramatic sweep as a portrait of an entire society. Essentially, though, the message is a familiar one: the ideals of the Mexican Revolution have been betrayed and the new Mexico is no less self-interested than the old one the Revolution sought to replace. What is perhaps different is the self-conscious attempt to link the new Mexico with its native tradition through the omnipresent figure of the mythical Ixca Cienfuegos, who seems to embody a communal ethic that is at odds with the rampant individualism of the modern world. Fuentes appears to be seeking here a new way for Mexico to imagine itself in a form that can also counter the homogenizing thrust of modernity. Yet the tension between nationalism and cosmopolitanism is never really fully resolved in Fuentes,[7] and it is perhaps this very tension that makes *La muerte de Artemio Cruz* a more interesting and internationally successful novel, oscillating as it does between Mexican specificity and wider speculation about humankind as a whole.

La muerte de Artemio Cruz uses the biography of one man to trace the course of modern Mexican history. Artemio Cruz goes from ardent revolutionary to corrupt capitalist, and his career exemplifies the direction that Mexico has taken since the Revolution. Again, there is nothing new in this, and the novel seems almost consciously to echo Mariano Azuela's *Los de abajo* (see chapter 2). As with the case of Solís and Cervantes in Azuela's classic novel, Fuentes' text dramatizes the death of idealism and the triumph of opportunism. Here Cruz shares a *villista* (supporters of Pancho Villa) prison cell with the disillusioned idealist Gonzalo Bernal. Bernal is executed, sacrificing himself for the principles he still believes in, while Cruz is set free after seemingly informing on his comrades to the enemy. Cruz subsequently uses his position as a revolutionary officer to enter into an alliance of convenience with a landowner (Bernal's father and representative of the very class against whom the Revolution was supposedly fought), a deal that provides the springboard for his future shady but lucrative career in politics and business. Mexico emerges as a country of 'chingones y pendejos', that is, either sons of bitches or poor bastards (there is a famous passage which parades the endless variations of the word 'chingar' ['to fuck'] in everyday Mexican speech), and in which the only rule is to screw others before they screw you.[8] If there is a new dimension to this social critique, it is the way the novel frames Cruz's career in the wider context of a cyclically recurrent pattern of Mexican history, in which the homeland is a 'desventurado país que a cada generación tiene que destruir a los antiguos poseedores y sustituirlos por nuevos amos, tan rapaces y ambiciosos como los anteriores' ('unfortunate country in which each generation has to destroy the old owners and replace them with new masters, just as rapacious and ambitious as the previous ones': p. 50). Historical allusions flesh out this idea, and the whole 'chingar' business portrays the nation as the angry and arrogant bastard offspring of a brutal, anonymous rape (the Spanish conquest).

The problem is that the apparently circular nature of history here does not seem to offer much hope for meaningful change. Even on his deathbed Cruz realizes that the cycle will continue, as he agonizes over the way his daughter's boyfriend is likely to inherit his estate and repeat the sequence of possession and dispossession all over again. Moreover, the ending of the novel juxtaposes Cruz's death with his childhood and birth. In the childhood episode, despite some language of idealization of the locale, the illegitimate Cruz is seen accidentally shooting his kind, gentle uncle. He is symbolically killing off a part of himself here and showing the first signs of the inheritance of his father's character, the meanest and most vicious member of the family. This suggests both determinism and the curse of fate. This is odd given that much of the novel seems to be built around the idea of choice and therefore moral responsibility. Cruz is always haunted by guilt because he failed to make the honourable choices in life that a number of contrasting characters, like Bernal, did. Yet now the implication is that he never really had a choice (and in fact elsewhere the novel has a number of pseudo-philosophical passages which could be read as presenting human choices as a process of narrowing down of options until freedom is restricted). Moreover, the juxtaposition of birth and death effectively tells us that Cruz's life is no more than an ephemeral, meaningless blip in the eternal scheme of things. Indeed the very fact that this novel is about a man's death as much as his life could be taken as an effective negation of life, and one of the final passages rather portentously places his life and death in the context of inevitable cosmic decay.

The ultimate effect of *La muerte de Artemio Cruz* is one of unresolved contradiction or, more generously, ambiguity. The novel brings out quite clearly the tension between the sort of existential and metaphysical scepticism that came to characterize much of the New Narrative, on the one hand, and the residual desire to offer effective social and political commentary on nationhood and Latin American reality, on the other. Fuentes' work never really manages to overcome this dichotomy. And in the end, *La muerte de Artemio Cruz* is probably most interesting not for what it has to say about Mexico, but for its embodiment of the ambiguity of reality. This, after all, is the implication of its narrative technique. It reads like a typical, if, in this case, rather mechanical, New Novel, with its fragmented structure, chronological inversions and variation on point of view. Most famously, the novel alternates third-person narrative with first- and second-person sections, which correspond, more or less, to the sensations of the dying man and the unconscious voice of his conscience. The technique is tiresome and clumsy, but at its best it conveys a sense of the complex and confusing nature of reality, and marks *La muerte de Artemio Cruz* as another example of the New Narrative's challenge to the idea of conventional realism.

Mario Vargas Llosa

A rather more winning example of the marriage of New Narrative technique to vision of reality is the work of Mario Vargas Llosa. He is the most consistently successful professional novelist to emerge from the Boom and has established a long and ongoing career as a much-translated and internationally recognized writer. He is also now one of the most vilified, largely because of his evolution from the youthful left to a more 'conservative' position that culminated in his failed candidacy for the presidency of Peru in 1990, after running on what has been described as a neo-liberal or even Thatcherite ticket. What this has to do with the quality of his writing is not clear (see chapter 7), but there can be no doubt that his work during the Boom period represents a huge literary achievement. As has been indicated, *La ciudad y los perros* can be regarded as marking the start of the Boom in 1962. But he also produced two other defining Boom novels in the same decade: *La casa verde* ('The Green House', 1966) and *Conversación en La Catedral* ('Conversation in The Cathedral', 1969). Moreover, he has gone on to produce a number of major novels, including, for example, two of Latin America's finest ever historical novels (or indeed novels of any kind): *La guerra del fin del mundo* ('The War of the End of the World', 1981), about the messianic peasant revolt led by Antônio Conselheiro in Brazil in 1897, and *La fiesta del chivo* ('The Feast of the Goat', 2000), about the dictatorship of Rafael Trujillo in the Dominican Republic and his assassination in 1961.

One thing above all sets Vargas Llosa apart from other practitioners of the New Novel. And that is that, by and large, he has always remained essentially a realist. The simple version of the New Narrative has it that it is a rejection of a so-called traditional realism. In practice, as has been seen, such a view, in its most reductive sense, is problematic. Vargas Llosa himself contributed to this perception of the New Novel by criticizing the simplistic outlook of broadly realist-oriented regional fiction and its slavish adherence to a presumed Latin American specificity.[9] However, unlike, say, Borges maybe, Vargas Llosa does not abandon the idea that the role of literature is to reflect reality. His complaint is simply that earlier fiction in Latin America did not do it very well. Instead of a narrow and misleadingly black-and-white version of realism, he sought to extend the parameters of realism to give a much fuller picture of reality that also captured its complexity and ambiguity. Hence his dream of a 'totalizing' novel that would present reality as a grand canvass, in all its multifaceted variety. But coupled with this is the desire to create an alternative fictional reality that will function as an exorcism of personal demons or obsessions. It is not the intention here to go into Vargas Llosa's theory of the novel in detail, but it is a fairly complex – if, for today's theoretical tastes, somewhat impressionistic – combination of the creation of fiction out of reality and the transformation of reality into fiction.[10]

Technique, then, is at the heart of Vargas Llosa's narrative, and he has always been regarded as a notoriously disciplined rather than artistically inspired writer. His approach depends on a number of key ideas: what he has called autonomous narrative, the *salto temporal* ('temporal leap') or *vasos comunicantes* ('communicating vessels'), and the *caja china* ('Chinese box'). All are linked. The aim of autonomous narrative is to create the sensation of a self-propelled narrative (sometimes linked to the idea of 'the disappearance of the author') in which the omniscient narrator or even author figure appears to withdraw, leaving the reader alone and face to face with an autonomous fictional reality, which he or she has to make sense of or interpret for himself or herself without obvious external guidance. The *caja china* basically refers to embedded or delegated points of view, where the characters themselves – rather than an external narrator – transmit thoughts, perceptions or narrative information, thus reminding the reader of the subjective and therefore varying nature of reality. Finally, the *vasos comunicantes* (of which the *salto temporal* is an element) involves the juxtaposition of episodes or dialogues from different times or places in such a way that each interacts with the other and thereby alters our perception of them: again, understanding of reality is extended without the need for direct narratorial intervention. Of course, autonomous narrative is an illusion. Indeed one might argue that the architectural complexity that the structuring of such a narrative entails actually draws attention to a masterful author figure manipulating the construction (this ultimate order would in the future form the basis of one of postmodernism's criticisms of modernism). However, the illusion often works, and the reader of Vargas Llosa's Boom narratives does get the sensation of a vast and complex reality and of sharing the characters' sense of confusion and disorientation in the face of that reality.

The technique is at a relatively embryonic stage in *La ciudad y los perros*, but is no less effective for that. The story – with semi-autobiographical elements – concerns the brutal treatment of young cadets at Lima's Leoncio Prado military academy (the novel caused a scandal and copies were subsequently burned outside the college). It tells the tale of the cadets' growing up both at the college and in the city beyond it, from which they come and into which they are eventually reabsorbed. The Spanish title, referring to the city and the cadets, already announces a realist heritage in that it clearly alludes to the human being's relationship to his or her environment. The college itself is like a microcosm of Peruvian society as a whole, with all the various ethnic and social groups represented. And the portrait of Lima (the original version included a map showing the geographical divisions of the capital) builds up a detailed picture of life in the different zones of the city. The broad social sweep, then, is that of a realist novel. What is different is the way the novel attempts to expand the reader's grasp of the reality depicted. For example, the *vasos comunicantes* technique (or early variations on it) means that one area is always seen in relation to another and the perceptions of characters from one social group always have to be compared to the differing perceptions of those from another. The main events of the novel, meantime, are told from the perspective of different characters, whom we also see in varying contexts and at varying times in their life. On top of that, characters are portrayed internally as well as externally, bringing out the gap between the inner self and the public projection of that self. For instance, in his internal monologues, the tough brute Boa comes across as a damaged boy who is only able to show his true emotions to a mongrel bitch. Most famously, the anonymous, timid and introspective narrator of some of the sections turns out near the end to be none other than the notorious school bully Jaguar. Thus a quite complex picture of reality emerges and the reader is forced to reflect actively on the conflict between appearance and reality.

Reality is fundamentally ambiguous, then. This is illustrated by the treatment of one of the novel's pivotal events. After a weak and tormented boy, nicknamed Esclavo or Slave, snitches on his fellow students, he is shot during a training exercise. One of the protagonists, Alberto, accuses Jaguar. This is the novel's key moral moment. Although the account of the boys' relationship to the city seems hugely deterministic (they are all moulded to conform to the system and each returns to his appropriate environment at the end), there is an emphasis on choice and responsibility. Alberto does not have the courage to see through the right moral choice, but gives in and withdraws his complaint when his comfortable future is threatened. Jaguar, however, does learn his lesson and, even if he does not transcend his social class, manages to change his life for the better and follow a more honest path than Alberto. But there is a massive ambiguity at the heart of this moral dilemma. It is never clarified who killed Esclavo. Reality remains unknowable in any complete sense.

Vargas Llosa's next novel, *La casa verde*, uses an interior rather than an urban setting, the small northern town of Piura and the jungle around the Marañón River. The author had lived in Piura as a child and had more recently visited and studied the jungle area in detail. There is another realist thrust here: to represent the jungle experience to an outside audience. The observation is often convincing, but more important is the intricate, multilayered narrative form (much more complex and confusing than the earlier novel) in which the reader becomes enmeshed. In other words, the formal experience of reading becomes akin to that of being in the jungle itself. But the matted, formal labyrinth is also an image of the corruption the jungle represents. In its tortuous, twisting account of at least five interrelated stories, the narrative builds up a bitter picture of hypocrisy and abuse, particularly with regard to the exploitation and degradation of the Indians at the hands of the supposed forces of 'civilization'.[11] The structure is itself a kind of formal equivalent of the moral quagmire that is life in the Peruvian interior. The title is important here. The green house is literally a brothel but also a metaphor for the jungle. The society depicted via formal asperity is thus projected as fundamentally degenerate.

Conversación en La Catedral exchanges a jungle labyrinth for an urban one, with Vargas Llosa's narrative technique now finely developed and reapplied to Lima, in a vast portrait of the decomposition of public and private life in Peru during the years of the military dictatorship of Manuel Odría (1948–56) and its aftermath (up to 1963). The conversation alluded to in the title is that which takes place in a bar, La Catedral, between a shabby near-dropout of a journalist, Santiago Zavala, and his oligarch father's former chauffeur, the poor black man Ambrosio Pardo. The conversation becomes the starting point for a densely entangled web of wide-ranging flashbacks that pessimistically captures the mood of the times across the social and political spectrum. Again, part of the function of the technique is to bring out a culture of concealment and hypocrisy. In this respect, an important revelation (deeply shocking to Santiago) is that Don Fermín, Zavala's respectable businessman father, regularly sodomized Ambrosio. Indeed the novel builds up an extensive picture of what is seen as sexual depravity, reflecting not only the corruption of the society of what is regularly referred to as a 'país jodido' ('a fucked-up country') but also its essential falseness. Though, as in *La casa verde*, there is some sense of irresolvable ambiguity, the effect of the narrative form is profoundly realistic, in that it captures the bewildering nature of life in a messy, chaotic and dishonest world.

Gabriel García Márquez

One of Vargas Llosa's great strengths as a writer is that he is a superb storyteller and produces some genuinely gripping narratives, despite their complexity. The last of the Big Four is an equally brilliant but very different kind of storyteller, more rooted in a rural oral tradition. He is also the writer most associated – rightly or wrongly – with Magical Realism, and author of what is widely regarded as the greatest Latin American novel of all time. The author is the 1982 Nobel Prize winner Gabriel García Márquez and the novel is *Cien años de soledad* ('One Hundred Years of Solitude', 1967).[12] *Cien años de soledad* raises issues about the relationship between literature and reality similar to those proposed in other examples of the New Narrative, but in a different – and therefore, according to perspective, richer or less consistent – way than Vargas Llosa.

The opening and closing of the novel provide clues. Near the start, the founder of the town and the dynasty that dominate the story's one hundred years, José Arcadio Buendía, is teaching his children how to read:

> En el cuartito apartado, cuyas paredes se fueron llenando poco a poco de mapas inverosímiles y gráficos fabulosos, les enseñó a leer y escribir y a sacar cuentas, y les habló de las maravillas del mundo no sólo hasta donde le alcanzaban sus conocimientos, sino forzando a extremos increíbles los límites de su imaginación.[13]

> (In the small room to the side, whose walls were filling up little by little with unrealistic maps and fabulous drawings, he taught them to read and write and do sums, and he spoke to them about the marvels of the world, not only up to the point his knowledge could reach, but forcing the limits of his imagination to incredible extremes.)

This seems to be an invitation to the reader not simply to read *Cien años de soledad* as a reflection of reality, but to create his or her own reality by using the free play of the imagination. Hence the presentation of a cube of ice in the first chapter. In the mind of father and children alike, the ice becomes a marvellous, magic, brilliant substance – a metaphor of the writing and reading process in which ordinary, raw material taken from reality can be transformed into something magical, or at least different, by the creative imagination.

The role of the gypsy Melquíades, who brings ice and other wonders to Macondo, is crucial to this process. For some critics, the final chapter seems to reveal that Melquíades is the narrator of the novel. Throughout the novel there have been numerous references to the incomprehensible manuscripts left behind by Melquíades, and at the end it is discovered that what these parchments tell is, in fact, the story of *Cien años de soledad*. So, when the last of the Buendías, Aureliano Babilonia, manages finally to decipher the manuscripts, he realizes that he is nothing more than a character in somebody else's narrative and that he will therefore disappear with the last line of the text. The novel seems to be foregrounding its own status as fiction, then, rather than as a conventional reflection of reality. This explains the element of fantasy in the novel (the primary manifestation of the break with realism). Quite simply, if this is a work of fiction, anything can happen. This is the key to the Magical Realist style – the most bizarre events are described in an absolutely natural manner.

However, if the novel challenges realism, this does not necessarily mean it rejects it outright. What *Cien años de soledad* may be doing is offering an alternative version of reality – that is, a specifically Latin American or even third world view in a cultural scene dominated by so-called first world perspectives. This is a more obviously political rendering of Carpentier's *lo real maravilloso* (see chapter 3). In García Márquez's novel, the 'fantastic' elements (such as a young girl ascending into heaven or a priest levitating after drinking a cup of hot chocolate) are presented as absolutely normal, while things like ice, magnets, false teeth, gramophones or movies seem utterly incredible. The distinction between reality and fantasy seems to be a matter of cultural assumptions, and what the novel does is to give voice to and privilege the point of view of a rural, isolated, and to some extent primitive community. The role of fantasy, then, may be to encourage a reinterpretation of reality in a way that defies conventional Eurocentric views of Latin America. The one-hundred-year time span of the novel is actually a compression of Latin American history from conquest and colonization, to Independence, 'progress' and 'democracy', to modern economic dependency. The subcontinent's history is repeatedly exposed as a series of essentially foreign myths that Latin America has internalized as its own history and identity. Discovery, the New World, the debt to Europe, Independence, freedom, progress, democracy and so forth are all fabricated (European or by extension North American) concepts which often have little to do with real human experience in Latin America. Hence Magical Realism can have a more subtle function. Magic represents the freedom of imagination, and imagination represents revolution: the novel is encouraging Latin

Americans to dare to imagine an alternative and, in fact, more real or authentic version of their own history and identity.

This is not, of course, unproblematic. This reading of Magical Realism has the same limitations as Carpentier's 'marvellous real'. The oral tradition is contained within a Western novelistic framework and, in the case of the ice, for example, there is a potentially dangerous complicity between educated author and reader who are fully aware that the dazzling diamond is no more than an ice cube. Giving voice to the ordinary folk may be no more than an illusion. And what about the overall dimension of the text's self-conscious fictionality? If literature is no more than fiction and reality itself is an illusion, then what is the meaning or value of commentary on socio-political reality?

A crucial episode in this respect is the massacre of the striking banana plantation workers. This is the crux of the novel's political level. Based on a real event, this is the story of how a North American fruit company has such economic power that it enjoys effective political influence and is able to get government troops to quash by force a strike. After the massacre of the workers, the bodies are removed and the killings are denied. Over time, the official version takes on the quality of truth and is even consecrated in the school history books. The implicit appeal to Latin Americans to challenge official versions of their history and make a stand for truth and authenticity is clear. But, when, in a notorious episode, the last of the Buendías – obsessed by the truth or otherwise of the massacre – asks the parish priest what he believes, the priest looks at him sceptically and replies: 'Ay, hijo . . . A mí me bastaría con estar seguro de que tú y yo existimos en este momento' ('Oh dear, my son . . . It would be enough for me if I could be sure that you and I exist at this very moment') (p. 354). A shocking note of radical doubt is introduced precisely at what seems to be a moment of truth. Indeed the novel is full of gloomy tales of hopelessness, death, lost dreams and shattered illusions, and often seems to repeat the sense of existential malaise that characterizes other examples of the New Narrative.

And so to the novel's ending, which really asks more questions than it answers. Macondo is destroyed by a 'biblical hurricane' and the Buendías are wiped off the face of the earth. This conclusion has been read as representing everything from the hope provided by the Cuban Revolution for a new era of change and justice to a pessimistic and apocalyptic vision of the hopelessness of the human condition.

Such ambiguity is central to the novel's richness and suggestiveness as literature, but surely a problem if it is to be read as an effective political commentary.

Other Writers of the Boom

The so-called Big Four were clearly the standard bearers for the New Novel and the most instrumental in its more cosmopolitan, international projection. But the 1960s also saw the production of major works by writers who had been associated with the rise of the New Narrative from the 1940s onwards (see chapter 3) and by others who were new to the scene. Of a more obviously existential bent were the works of Juan Carlos Onetti and Ernesto Sábato.

Onetti's main novels of this period were *Juntacadáveres* (tr. 'Body Snatcher', 1964) and its sequel (though written earlier) *El astillero* ('The Shipyard', 1961). Both feature a character called Larsen, a sort of grubby existential anti-hero, whose struggles and failures reveal a peculiar nobility of spirit in the face of the smug small-mindedness of the community of Santa María in which the novels are set. Larsen's scheme to open a brothel in the town is described as a vocation, an ideal, a statement of faith. But though it rubs the noses of the local bourgeoisie in their own hypocrisy, the plan is none the less an ironic inversion of the ideals of the realist hero of the vocational novel, and its failure a symbol of the frustrated quest for purpose in life. The same is the case with his plan in the 1961 novel to take over a local shipyard and marry the owner's daughter. His faith in his project is contradicted by the facts that the shipyard is bankrupt and ruined, while the woman is an unstable young virgin who wants nothing to do with Larsen and finds the sexual act repellent. He eventually succumbs to madness and death. Larsen's ambiguity makes him a kind of emblematic character of the New Narrative, intriguing and non-conformist, yet sordid, repulsive and doomed to inevitable failure.

Darker still is Sábato's *Sobre héroes y tumbas* ('On Heroes and Tombs', 1961). Here Fernando Olmos suffers from a paranoid fear of the blind, and sinks into self-destruction as he immerses himself in an infernal underworld inhabited by an evil blind sect, the climax of which is his own – as it is presented – vile act of sexual intercourse with a blind woman. Moreover, he is killed by the daughter with whom he had committed incest, another metaphorical expression of negativity and the fall from grace. This inversion of traditional values is brought out by a narrative form characterized by distortion or fragmentation of chronology and point of view, something which made Sábato quite an influential figure for aspiring practitioners of the New Narrative.

Writers like Alejo Carpentier and the Neo-Indigenist José María Arguedas, meantime, sought to maintain a more social and political focus while still renovating narrative form. Carpentier's *El siglo de las luces* (tr. 'Explosion in a Cathedral', 1962) is one of Latin America's great historical novels, though not perhaps typical of the New Novel as a whole. Set between 1791 and 1808, it concerns the French Revolution and the attempts to export it to the Caribbean. Another tale of the betrayal of revolutionary ideals, it charts the way fanaticism leads to tyranny and injustice in Guadeloupe and Cayenne, with the revolutionary Victor Hugues ending up as a slave-master despite returning to the Caribbean to liberate slaves. Yet two central symbols bring out the ambiguous perspective on history. The exportation of the guillotine is a sign of the terrible human cost of change but also a path towards the creation of an ideal. Similarly, a painting of a cathedral in mid-explosion is an image of destruction but also of incomplete, ongoing transformation. History, though circular, is thus a stuttering and imperfect process towards improvement. This positive trend is concluded in Carpentier's 1978 celebration of the Cuban Revolution, *La consagración de la primavera* ('The Rite of Spring').

Arguedas' novels of the Boom decade display a similar mixture of the positive and the uncertain. *Todas las sangres* ('All Bloods', 1964) is a panoramic view of Andean society in the 1950s during a period of social and economic change. In it the indigenous population become a skilled workforce, resort to strike action and take over the running of the land themselves. In other words, they manage to advance and adapt while remaining true to their indigenous identity. However, though his last novel, *El zorro de arriba y el zorro de abajo* ('The Fox Above and the Fox Below', published posthumously in 1971), seems to posit a process of positive transculturation between coastal society (*abajo*) and that of the Andes (*arriba*), it also shows the annihilation of indigenous values by capitalism in its withering portrait of the industrialized port of Chimbote. Indeed, while the novel tries to direct traditional oral forms of expression in new ways, it actually ends up as a kind of monstrous and directionless labyrinth. The book was never finished and Arguedas took his own life in 1969.

The first novel of the Paraguayan Augusto Roa Bastos, *Hijo de hombre* ('Son of Man'), from 1960, has a similar vision to that of Arguedas, though it focuses more explicitly on revolutionary guerrilla war than on possibly fanciful theories of transculturation. Like other Latin American novels, it is built around the inversion of traditional Christian imagery, so that salvation is placed in the hands of the common man (a literal rather than Christian 'son of man'), in this case the Guaraní-speaking peasantry. The novel sees Paraguay as a kind of fallen paradise and offers a series of Christ figures representative of a hoped-for redemption. The most important is the aptly named Cristóbal Jara (his name echoing that of Christ in Spanish), who dies while bringing into the desert life-saving water for a 'sinner' (the traitor Miguel Vera) during the Chaco War (1932–5). Despite death, Jara seems to undergo a kind of metaphorical resurrection by continuing to inspire others through the power of his example: 'El camión de Cristóbal Jara no atravesó la muerte para salvar la vida de un traidor. Envuelto en llamas sigue rodando en la noche, sobre el desierto, en las picadas, llevando el agua para la sed de los sobrevivientes' ('Cristóbal Jara's truck did not cross death just to save the life of a traitor. Covered in flames, it continues rolling through the night, across the desert, along the trails, carrying water to relieve the thirst of the survivors').[14] But Jara achieves nothing in practical terms and the other Christ figures in the novel are often cast in a doubtful or negative light. The ambiguity is only increased by the enclosing of a protest narrative in the packaging of a kind of Magical Realism and New Narrative structural fragmentation.

Defenders of Roa Bastos would argue that his ambiguity is functional. In his massive dictator novel of 1974, for instance, *Yo el Supremo*, about the extraordinary regime of Dr José Gaspar Rodríguez de Francia (1766–1840), the dizzying web of interlocking narrative voices could be seen actually to encode liberty in that the novel's very discourse becomes a challenge to monolithic or authoritarian versions of reality. If so, Roa represents a constructive resolution of political commentary and New Novelistic technique. Others, however, might see the verbose impenetrability of the later novel as a barrier to effective political comment and a reminder of the fundamentally elusive nature of history and reality.

The Last Novel of the Boom?

The difficulties of matching politics to a new understanding of fiction's problematic relation to reality were probably responsible for the ultimate exhaustion of the Boom. Increasingly the sort of New Novel associated with the Boom would come to be seen as an unnecessarily complex expression of modernist elitism and anxiety at loss of order. What is sometimes regarded (notwithstanding the caveats about dating mentioned at the beginning of this chapter) as the last major novel of the Boom could be seen as a last hurrah of this dual tendency towards complexity and scepticism.

José Donoso's *El obsceno pájaro de la noche*, published in 1970, is one of the most technically demanding and existentially despairing of the Boom novels. Donoso was an important figure operating on the fringes of the Big Four, and 1970 marked the culmination of his own ambition to become a fully integrated member of the Boom club.[15] The lengthy narrative of *El obsceno pájaro de la noche* is delivered in a tortuously fragmented and distorted form, largely from the standpoint of its schizophrenic protagonist Humberto Peñaloza, also known as Mudito. The plot barely merits summarizing and it all ends depressingly with Mudito being sewn up inside an accumulation of sacks and cast on to a fire by an old crone, where he is burnt to cinders. The novel, it seems, is wilfully negative and bewildering. One explanation is, of course, that the narrator is mad, but madness may also be a truer reflection of the chaos of reality. When he lives alone with 'monsters' (the hideously deformed), Mudito reflects that 'un único ser normal en un mundo de monstrous adquiere *él* la categoría de fenómeno al ser *anormal*, transformándolos a ustedes (los monstruos) en normales' ('a sole normal being in a world of monsters acquires *himself* the status of a phenomenon by being *abnormal*, transforming you [the monsters] into the normal').[16] The mad or the monstrous is merely a question of perspective, and Mudito links this explicitly to literature when he rejects the 'aspiraciones de esos escritorzuelos que creían en la existencia de *una realidad* que retratar' ('aspirations of those scribblers who used to believe in the existence of *a reality* that could be portrayed') (p. 242).

Whether this is a renunciation of all logocentric discourse or a more precisely metaphysical expression of anguish, the novel becomes the complete literary embodiment of a reality that is emptied of all sense or meaning. It systematically dissolves all binary distinctions so that conventional logic is fully eroded and order is constantly transformed into chaos. The lower-middle-class Humberto's descent into the persona of the crazed odd-job man Mudito is one manifestation of this, as are the disintegration of his boss, Don Jerónimo de Azcoitía, into 'un ser retorcido, horripilante, monstruoso' ('a twisted, horrifying, monstrous creature') (p. 506), and the metamorphosis of his beautiful wife Inés into the wrinkled and disgusting hag and witch Peta Ponce. Any notion of order here is no more than a fragile human construct. In Donoso, the complete and utter negation of meaning and the nihilistic implosion of the representative function of literature take the uncertainty or scepticism inherent in the Boom to an extreme endgame of no return. What comes next will have to be change. Cue the emergence of the Post-Boom.

CHAPTER 5

After the Boom

The New Novel in Latin America did not fade away with the end of the Boom, and there has been a rich and varied pattern of literary production in the region by both experienced and newer writers from the later 1960s up to the beginning of the twenty-first century. However, a perceived critical clarity about the nature of the Boom has not yet been matched by a similar sense of clarity about what came after it. Though there have indeed been many lively debates about the nature of the New Narrative and the Boom in Latin American fiction, there is now something approaching a broad consensus as to their chronology and characteristics. Such a consensus is more elusive when it comes to the rather more slippery category of the so-called Post-Boom, a term that has come to be used to refer to developments from the late 1960s and early 1970s onwards. Indeed, as late as 1990, a leading critic of the work of Argentina's Manuel Puig (1932–90) (linked by many with the emergence of a Post-Boom) was complaining of the way in which 'critics were quick to produce a new category . . . variously – and infelicitously – designated the "*petit*-Boom", the "Junior Boom", or even the "post-Boom" '.[1] However, the very currency of such terms does seem to indicate that some perceptible change of sorts was under way from around 1970, even if it was difficult to define clearly what that change really constituted.

There are, for example, definite changes in material circumstances around this time which alert us to the possibility of a shift in emphasis. A number of major novelists associated with the Boom noticeably develop in a somewhat different direction during and after the seventies. And a cohort of new writers with a conspicuously different voice or agenda begin to publish around the turn of these key decades. As time goes on, authors begin to articulate consciously the sense of a break with the sixties, while a younger generation emerges whose members specifically define themselves in terms of a rupture or break with the past (the 'past' now being not the supposedly traditional realist and regional novel against which the Boom was seen as a climactic reaction, but as something embodied in the canonized *nueva novela* of the Boom itself). But, of course, thirty years is a long time (compared to the ten years often used to characterize the Boom): yet, at the beginning of the twenty-first century, critics are still talking about a Post-Boom phase in Latin American fiction (principally Spanish American, though there are some commonalities with the situation in Brazil[2]). Surely such a lengthy period cannot elicit the same degree of critical consensus or coherence as has been identified in the Boom.

This raises one of the problems of the notion of a Post-Boom. The term only has true meaning when it is used to refer, literary-historically speaking, to that which came after the Boom. But, of course, that could mean anything. The nature of the transition from Boom to Post-Boom is, in any case, as fuzzy as it is clear, and a very wide range of differing kinds of approaches to fiction has come to be encompassed under the latter umbrella term. As with the term 'postmodernism' (with which the Post-Boom is sometimes, polemically, identified), which is a marker both of a break with modernism and of a reconfiguration of it, it is perhaps helpful to understand the Post-Boom not only as that which follows the Boom but also as a new attitude towards the experimental New Novel associated with the Boom. The Post-Boom will then emerge both as a rejection of the New Narrative and as a new version of it, a sort of 'new' New Novel. Moreover, and in keeping with the idea of changing attitudes towards fictional phenomena, it must be remembered that the concept of a Post-Boom evolves during a period of commodification of the Latin American novel in the global market, the fetishization of certain types of Latin American writing by the universities or the academy in the USA and Europe, the rise of literary theory, the politicization of literary criticism, and the growth of cultural studies (see chapter 7). Defining the Post-Boom thus becomes a matter of political choice as much as one of literary history, and its perception and use or manipulation as a term become as important as any sense of its underlying literary-historical validity. Any consideration of the Post-Boom, then, will have to tread a fine line between explaining it as a reality or true phenomenon (in the sense that the Boom was) and maintaining an awareness of the fundamental fluidity and porosity of it as a category.

The End of the Boom?

The idea of the existence of the Post-Boom depends on that of the demise of the Boom. In literary terms, as will be seen, this involves, very broadly speaking, the exhaustion of experimentalism and a return to an engagement with human reality. But the climate of change can be identified first in the extra-textual context of the material world outside of literary discourse. The end of the Boom is connected to two external phenomena or events. The first relates to the world of publishing. The New Novel may have been an evolving trend since the 1940s or earlier, but the Boom was really (as the word 'boom' implies) a finite burst of commercial activity. For many, the Spanish American Boom actually took place in Europe, and was particularly promoted by the Barcelona publishing house Seix Barral, which, with its canny combination of international novelists' conventions and literary prizes, sought to expand its market. This publishing house is sometimes credited with being an engine of the Boom, particularly via its foundational discovery and publication of *La ciudad y los perros* and the award in 1962 of its highly prestigious Biblioteca Breve Prize to that novel's author, Mario Vargas Llosa (see chapter 4). Seix Barral also, in 1965, started up the series Nueva Narrativa Hispánica, reinforcing the sense of coherence, importance and international identity of the Spanish American New Narrative, now in some ways the voice of the Spanish-speaking world. However, by the end of the decade, there was a major split within Seix Barral and the key player, writer, publisher and entrepreneur Carlos Barral, left to found Barral Editores in 1970 (though its Barral Prize fizzled out after only four years).

The Biblioteca Breve Prize was suspended in 1970, and the novel which would have otherwise certainly been given the award in that year, José Donoso's *El obsceno pájaro de la noche* (see chapter 4), marks both the high point and the end of the Boom. This novel has been seen as representing the culmination of the process of complexity, fragmentation, tortuousness and sheer difficulty that had come to be viewed as synonymous with the Boom, but also as the extreme of experimentalism, the point of exhaustion and no return. In the words of one critic: 'Con esta novela se cierra y se cumple un ciclo, más allá del cual no existe otra posibilidad expresiva . . . [L]a novela de Donoso es el broche que cierra una etapa, después de la cual sólo cabe cambiar de rumbo' ('With this novel a cycle is both completed and closed, beyond which no other possibility of expression exists . . . Donoso's novel snaps shut one stage, after which the only thing to do is change direction').[3] Donoso would himself later assert the need for a sharp change in direction, and certainly saw the schism at Seix Barral as one indicator of the end of the Boom and as a factor in the halting of its promotion as a concept (Donoso 1983, pp. 89–90).

Donoso also links the events at Seix Barral with a turning point in the Cuban Revolution (the so-called 'caso Padilla' or Padilla affair), the other main external matter pointing up the end of the Boom (Donoso 1983, pp. 89–90). The Cuban Revolution was actually an important factor in the Boom. It is often said that the revolution created a sense of political unity amongst Latin American writers, but this is only true in part – after all, it has frequently been noted that one of the main features of the New Narrative is the tendency to accent 'universal' (so-called) existential scepticism despite the backdrop of specifically Latin American contexts (see chapters 3 and 4). Oddly enough, what the Cuban Revolution did for the New Novel was to make it fashionable and enhance its marketability, bringing Latin America to international public consciousness and creating an appetite for the consumption of Latin American texts. It probably also created a sense or illusion of community or solidarity amongst Latin American writers wishing to believe in the reality of a boom in the cultural projection of their region. However, the 1971 arrest and subsequent humiliation of the Cuban poet Heberto Padilla, on the grounds of being allegedly counter-revolutionary, led to a huge rift between Latin American writers and shattered the mirage of the unity of the Boom. Donoso again: 'si en algo tuvo unidad casi completa el *boom* . . . fue en la fe primera en la causa de la revolución cubana; creo que la desilusión producida por el caso Padilla la desbarató, y desbarató la unidad del *boom*' ('if there was any sense in which there was complete unity in the Boom . . . it was in the fundamental faith in the Cuban Revolution; I think that the disillusionment caused by the Padilla affair destroyed it, and destroyed the unity of the Boom itself') (Donoso 1983, p. 46).

It is obvious with hindsight that by the beginning of the 1970s a phase was drawing to a close. The Post-Boom, perhaps in an only gradually tangible way, was one of the signs of a reaction to this sense of an end of an era.

Of course, the idea of an 'end of an era' is simply brought into sharper focus by the aforementioned external factors: the deeper reasons for it are internal, literary ones. The New Novel of the Boom was, to put it crudely, running out of steam by around 1970. The Boom as an idea was predicated on the notion of newness: the New Novel's appeal lay precisely in its shock value, the radical jolting and challenging of reader expectations grounded in traditional realism. Yet by 1970 features such as fantasy, multiple narrative voices and structural fragmentation had become the norm, effectively *de rigueur* features of any fat new Spanish American novel aspiring to inter-national recognition. A new orthodoxy had essentially been created, and it was inevitable that authors would react against it as writers had previously against realism. Donoso once more, commenting on his own fiction after 1970:

> Lo que me interesa . . . es hacer una batida contra la aceptada novela clásica: no la novela clásica antigua sino la contemporánea . . . Es decir la novela que bajo el disfraz de una libertad narrativa forja una serie de reglas de las cuales no es posible prescindir. Por ejemplo, todas las reglas terribles que me parece que usa Cortázar: *Rayuela* es un muestrario de reglas encubiertas que forjan toda una teoría de la novela: esta teoría pretende destruir la novela clásica pero forja otra novela clásica.[4]

> (What interests me . . . is to take a potshot at the accepted classical novel: not the old-style classical novel but the contemporary one . . . That is, the kind of novel which, operating under the disguise of narrative freedom, forges a whole series of rules which it is not possible to do without. For example, all those terrible rules which, it seems to me, that Cortázar uses: *Hopscotch* is a catalogue of covert rules that forge an entire theory of the novel: this theory seeks to destroy the classical novel but instead forges another kind of classical novel.)

To maintain any sense of freshness or even effectiveness, the New Novel would therefore need to turn against what was beginning to seem a kind of rapidly fossilizing, wilful, narrative complexity or obscur-ity. This rebellion would take many forms, but would often boil down to some combination of: a return to some form of traditional structures, an embracing of or engagement with mass or popular culture, and an increased orientation towards social or political reality.

A Post-Boom

This happened in two broad ways: first, via the emergence a new group (sometimes, a little fancifully maybe, referred to as a new generation) of writers, the most notable of whom was probably Manuel Puig; second, via a startling change in direction in the work of already established writers, most notably perhaps Donoso and Vargas Llosa. However, before moving on to consider these developments, it is important to note that the seeds of this change were already well and truly present within the Boom itself.

The literary coherence of the Boom is questionable anyway. The so-called Big Four of Cortázar, Fuentes, García Márquez and Vargas Llosa are as different as they are similar. Despite the use of fantasy and fragmentation as well as critical claims of existential uncertainty, all offer commentaries on Latin American politics and society. Moreover, García Márquez's *Cien años de soledad* – despite being considered by many as the culmination and the great novel of the Boom – has relatively little of the structural complexity of the work of the other authors mentioned, and has a distinctly popular tone and content: published in 1967, it is really a pivotal work marking the transition from Boom to Post-Boom. It contains many of the features that some commentators would see as typical of the Boom: in particular a radical questioning of the nature of reality and literature's ability to describe it, coupled with a distinct whiff of metaphysical malaise or even pessimism. Yet if there is a lot of repetition of names and talk of circular time, the reader experiences events through a relatively easily digestible and largely linear narrative framework, which deals with an ordinary rural culture in an often down-to-earth and perfectly entertaining way, and offers a fairly obvious socio-political reading of everyday Latin American reality. The novel, in other words, posits a complex literary-intellectual problematization of the relationship between literature and reality, while at the same time seeking to demystify reality and put forward a popular and in some ways authentically Latin American demystification of literature and reality.

In a similar, if converse, way, Guillermo Cabrera Infante's (Cuba, 1929–) *Tres tristes tigres* (tr. 'Three Trapped Tigers'), with its playful punning on pop culture, should be and often is linked clearly to the Post-Boom, yet was published two years before *Cien años de soledad*, in 1965, and has much of the same tone and structural qualities as *Rayuela*, Cortázar's massively experimental Boom novel *par excellence*. Political and apolitical at the same time, *Tres tristes tigres* is characterized by linguistic games, allusions to movies and a love of nightlife, but is equally profoundly difficult and elusive. What *Cien años de soledad* and *Tres tristes tigres* illustrate is the fact that any shift to a Post-Boom is not as sudden or as radical as it might seem: as with most patterns of literary evolution, the process is a gradual, accretive, subtle one (and therefore, too, at the other end of the process, probably still ongoing as well).

New writers: Manuel Puig

None the less, despite the preceding caveats, a marked sense of change was in the air by the late 1960s, and this owed much to the emergence of a string of new writers, the most prominent and successful of whom was Manuel Puig. His *Boquitas pintadas* (tr. 'Heartbreak Tango'), which appeared in 1969, is the landmark text in the transition to the Post-Boom. In distinction from the supposed elitism of some Boom novels, Puig's novel gained popularity across certain perceived class and educational divides (though so, of course, did *Cien años de soledad*). It was about ordinary people, set in unglamorous, small-town Argentina amongst the *cursi* or 'vulgar' lower middle classes. Moreover, its cultural allusions were specifically to mass and popular culture. Together with its companion piece of a year earlier, *La traición de Rita Hayworth* (tr. 'Betrayed by Rita Hayworth', 1968), Puig's work told its story via a reworking of old Hollywood movies, romantic fiction, soap operas or *radionovelas*, and the slushy lyrics of popular songs such as tangos. Indeed the titles of the first two novels refer to a Hollywood star who came to prominence in the 1940s and to a tango lyric.

If all this implies accessibility, however, the reality is a little more problematic. *Boquitas pintadas* was subtitled a *folletín*, a term suggesting it would have the tone of a serial or melodrama: and to some extent it does. However, the narrative form is really an echo of the so-called autonomous narrative of the Boom (see chapter 4): instead of a third-person narrator, the plot is advanced via diary entries, letters, newspaper announcements, various listings and even stream-of-consciousness passages. And if popular culture is to some degree embraced, its effects are also critiqued: the characters here are constructed in their tedious conformism by mass culture, while the fantasies such culture generates are doomed to failure – the first novel's title actually alludes to the treacherous nature of the Hollywood dream, and the second's hint of sex and glamour (it is a shortened form of 'Boquitas pintadas de rojo carmesí' ['Lips painted with crimson red lipstick']) gives way to 'the unpalatable truth behind all illusions' (Bacarisse in Swanson 1990, p. 211) in the form of the epigraph to the second part, 'Boquitas azules, violáceas, negras' ('Lips that are blue, purplish, black').

This same tension can be seen in Puig's most famous, and more explicitly political, novel, *El beso de la mujer araña* ('Kiss of the Spider Woman', 1976). Once again, the text is structured around an interplay between, according to one's assessment of it, an awkward or productive exchange between bolero lyrics and the narration of B-movies on the one hand, and, on the other, a showy attempt at autonomous narrative based on dialogue, reports, footnotes and stream of consciousness. The problem is that the novel seems both to recuperate and to repudiate both popular mass culture and serious high-modernist narration. This links to its relationship to politics and human reality. The protagonists are two male prisoners sharing a cell, one there because of political activism, the other because of a homosexual liaison with a minor. The former is associated with 'serious' culture, the latter with 'popular' culture. As the unlikely pair come closer together, the idea develops that sexual repression is at the heart of all repression, and that the sexually repressed must become more politicized while the politically aware must become more sensitive to human limitations.

Connected with this is a dual notion: first, the sense that mass culture conditions individuals to play out their social roles in a way that fundamentally represses them, while, second, it at the same time provides an escape or liberation, as well as real human insight and an outlet for emotion denied by the asceticism of certain brands of political commitment. At one stage, the cell-mates argue over a romantic thriller which turns out to be a Nazi propaganda film: the difficulty is that while the film is an obvious example of manipulation through popular culture, the narrative itself is hugely enjoyable and completely interchangeable (if the affiliations of the heroes and villains were simply altered) with a more standard movie, this suggesting in part that film and narrative are no more than that and can never hope to capture reality. It seems that this is a Post-Boom novel seeking to achieve a more direct engagement with socio-political reality, while simultaneously problematizing the relationship between fiction and reality *à la* Boom. In this sense, the Post-Boom is as much the new face of the New Novel of the Boom as it is its replacement.

Change and established writers

This feeling of change and continuity is underlined by the fact that the other key marker of the transition to a Post-Boom is the transformation in the work of established writers who made their name in association with the Boom. The turn to the popular is striking: Vargas Llosa turns his hand to farce and soap opera; Donoso adopts the style of erotica, mysteries and transparent realism; Fuentes writes a tongue-in-cheek spy thriller (*La cabeza de la hidra* ['The Hydra Head', 1978); García Márquez produces a kind of detective novel (*Crónica de una muerte anunciada* ['Chronicle of a Death Foretold', 1981] and later a nostalgic sentimental romance (*El amor en los tiempos del cólera* ['Love in the Time of Cholera', 1985]).

Vargas Llosa and Donoso are perhaps the best examples. The Peruvian's *Pantaleón y las visitadoras* (tr. 'Captain Pantoja and the Special Service', 1973) is a sexual comedy, which uses the structures of autonomous narrative in a much more accessible way. Equally entertaining (and an international hit) was his *La tía Julia y el escribidor* ('Aunt Julia and the Scriptwriter') from 1977. In a style reminiscent of Puig, Vargas Llosa tells an autobiographical coming-of-age story in counterpoint to accounts of an increasingly bizarre series of radio soap operas. If anything, though, despite a clear level of social satire, there is a diminution here in the political content of his work or at least in the strength of political engagement. Moreover, both the military and the 'people' are mocked in the earlier text, while the later one charts the autobiographical rise to authority of the mature, serious author against the background of the breakdown and eventual undoing of his former senior colleague, the writer of popular pot-boiler radio serials. The formal conversion to the popular is not matched, then, and may even be countered by content that might be taken as the embodiment of a position of elitism.

Donoso is more explicit about overcoming the perceived elitism of the Boom, despite his earlier aspiration to and eventual attachment to it. He sees the New Novel as 'un callejón sin salida' ('a blind alley') and asks (in 1982): '¿No ha llegado un momento de ruptura para la novela latinoamericana contemporánea, de cambio, para renacer de las cenizas de tantas y tantas novelas totalizadoras, agobiantes de significado, ahogantes de experimentos, que se imprimen todos los días?' ('Hasn't there come a moment of rupture for the contemporary Latin American novel, of change, so that it can be reborn from the ashes of so, so many totalising novels, oppressive with meaning, suffocating with experimentation, that are printed every day?').[5] His *Casa de campo* ('A House in the Country', 1978) openly eschews the idea, so dear to practitioners of and commentators on the New Novel, of the 'disappearance of the author' (similar to 'autonomous narrative'), and instead adopts a style which foregrounds and lays bare the workings of a narratorial-cum-authorial figure, who declares at one stage that 'en la hipócrita no-ficción de las ficciones en que el autor pretende eliminarse siguiendo reglas preestablecidas por otras novelas, o buscando fórmulas narrativas novedosas . . . , veo un odioso puritanismo que estoy seguro que mis lectores no encontrarán en mi escritura' ('in that hypocritical non-fiction of those fictions in which the author seeks to remove himself by following pre-existing rules established by other novels, or by trying to find fancy new narrative formulae . . . , I see an odious kind of puritanism which I am sure my readers will not find in my writing').[6]

On top of this, the novel is a pretty transparent political allegory of the Allende government and the Pinochet military coup in Chile in the 1970s. Yet the new technique of the deliberate foregrounding of authorial machinations actually draws attention to the fictionality of the text and in so doing (apart from problematizing the political application of the allegory) emphasizes what was really the central contention of the New Novel of the Boom: that reality cannot be faithfully captured by literature. Donoso is thus a perfect illustration of the Post-Boom as being not simply a rejection of the Boom, but also a fresh reformulation of some of its core tenets. And this is what much of his fiction of the 1970s and 1980s does.

For instance, *La misteriosa desaparición de la marquesita de Loria* ('The Mysterious Disappearance of the Marquise of Loria', 1980) subverts literature and reality from within, by seducing the reader into the easy comfort of a popular narrative style (with elements of, amongst other things, documentary, detective mystery and soft porn), only to pull the rug out from under his or her feet by undermining the apparent pattern of narrative progress and leaving us with an inexplicable and unsettling mystery: the formal opposite of the attempted shock tactics of the seemingly chaotic *El obsceno pájaro de la noche*, then, achieves an exactly similar effect. The very interplay between Boom and Post-Boom is played out formally too in a semi-autobiographical tale that is actually about the phenomenon of the New Novel: *El jardín de al lado* ('The Garden Next Door', 1981). What seems a straightforward realist account of frustrated male author Julio Méndez's attempt to write the Chilean *Rayuela* and gain access to the hallowed ranks of the Boom authors is thoroughly overturned by a startling final chapter, in which the narrator reveals herself to be the seemingly feeble wife of Julio. Literary representation ends up being the opposite of what we thought it was and realist principles are undermined by a New Narrative style based on the manipulation rather than outright destruction of realism. *El jardín de al lado*, a satire of the publishing scene for Spanish American writers, trumpets the death of the New Novel at the very same time as it renovates it: it is both a break with the past and the elaboration of an intimate connection to it.

Versions of the Post-Boom

The tension between Boom and Post-Boom noted above has led one of the key commentators on both phenomena to think in terms of a transitional phase. In Shaw's reading of, for example, Puig, the Argentine writer, with his mixture of scepticism and political engagement, is essentially a transitional figure (Shaw 1998, p. 37). However, the idea of a 'transition' implies the existence of a clear Post-Boom proper. Shaw seems to identify this with 'a renewal of interest in referentiality . . . [,] reader friendliness, plot centeredness, the return to the here and now of Spanish America' (Shaw 1998, p. 49). Hence Shaw's championing of Chile's Antonio Skármeta (1940–) as one of the major embodiments of the values of the Post-Boom.[7]

Skármeta certainly articulates in his essays a kind of manifesto for a Post-Boom, proposing a type of writing that is self-consciously in opposition to the Boom, anti-elitist, accessible, concerned with the everyday, socially committed and generally positive.[8] He can also be seen as producing a series of novels that embody this type of writing – plot-centred and clearly structured works like: *Soñé que la nieve ardía* ('I Dreamt the Snow was Burning', 1975), with its use of the mass cultural metaphor of soccer to explore a self-interested young man's growing and partly transformative relationship with ordinary, mutually supportive working-class people; *La insurrección* ('The Uprising', 1982), a celebration of the revolutionary movement of Sandinismo via an account of a revolt against the Somoza regime in Nicaragua; and *Ardiente paciencia* ('Burning Patience', 1985), a story of love and poetry built partly around a postman's relationship with the great Chilean poet Pablo Neruda, but used as a backdrop for an exploration of the overturning of a potentially joyous Allende era by the dark days of the Pinochet dictatorship.

None the less, some may feel that Skármeta, if well known, is not quite as major (and therefore as representative) a figure as Shaw perhaps paints him. Moreover, the picture of the Post-Boom that the Chilean proposes may not totally correspond to the reality, which is often a lot more ambiguous. Shaw himself effectively acknowledges this. He notes, for instance, the apparent existence of a very different kind of Post-Boom associated with writers like Cuba's Severo Sarduy (1937–93) and Mexico's Salvador Elizondo (1932–) (Shaw 1998, p. 49). Though there is a degree of change in their later work, both these writers are obsessed with language and textual self-referentiality – the opposite of a Post-Boom embodied in Skármeta, and really an extreme version of the doubt about the relationship between fiction and external reality that characterized the New Novel linked with the Boom. Indeed a key influence here is Cuba's José Lezama Lima (1910–76) and his 1966 novel *Paradiso* (a work that can probably best be situated as adjacent to rather than part of the Boom), which is built around a near hermetic philosophy of poetics expressed in what is often described as a Neobaroque style.

Sarduy is the more famous of the inheritors of Lezama Lima's barely penetrable version of the Baroque. His best-known novels are *De donde son los cantantes* (tr. 'From Cuba with a Song', 1967) and *Cobra* (1972). Neither has any real narrative in a conventional sense.

In the first, the main characters (such as they are) seek their own meaning, but meaning is endlessly deferred; and plot (such as it is) is merely 'dictated by phonetic associations or by the internal logic of language itself'.[9] The mutational or seemingly free-associational structure is even more extreme in *Cobra*, where a transvestite stripper is male and female, dead and alive, wax doll and human, and moves with a bunch of bikers from Europe to India in order to join up with an oriental deity. Sarduy, a student of Roland Barthes, is clearly putting into novelistic practice some of the theoretical precepts of structuralism and post-structuralism where 'writing' is merely a string of signifiers in a state of flight, with no ultimate meaning behind them, and is therefore no more than the very act of writing ('el acto de escribir'[10]) itself. The sexual dimension of *Cobra* underlines this idea: the erotic here is a ludic game, which, like language, is perceived as wonderfully and lavishly wasteful and ultimately non-productive in its limitless pursuit of pleasure.[11]

Although in its non-utilitarian playfulness *Cobra* explicitly rejects the Boom and has been described as 'a work of the anti-Boom',[12] it has obvious connections with it too: nobody could deny, for example, the ludic quality of, say, Cortázar in the 1960s – Sarduy's work is (in part at least) just a radical extension of that ludic dimension into a more complete and absolute rupturing of the notion of writing as a generator of meaning. In other words, Sarduy represents a refocusing or repositioning of some of the ideas behind the New Novel of the Boom as much as he represents its rejection or destruction.

This is an important point. The notion of a transition may be slightly misleading. If Skármeta represents a kind of Post-Boom proper, this implicitly takes the meaning of the term 'Post-' to refer to that which is in opposition to and comes after the Boom. But perhaps a more fundamental meaning of the term 'Post-' is to posit simply a new attitude to or relationship with that which is being followed or superseded. There has been much debate about the connections or differences between the Post-Boom and concepts such as postmodernism or postcolonialism (see Shaw 1998). In fact the relationship between the Boom and Post-Boom could be seen usefully to echo that between modernism and postmodernism in the sense that the latter is not simply a rejection of the former but merely a new approach to it (just as postcolonialism is new way of understanding, thinking about and relating to colonialism rather than a plain assertion of its demise). In this sense, Sarduy and Puig, for instance, would be key figures of the Post-Boom rather than only transitional ones. This would help to resolve the tension in Shaw's argument between 'the mainstream element in the Post-Boom [, which] is a tendency back to referentiality' and a Post-Boom that is 'a continuum that runs from extreme documentality/testimoniality to patterns of writing in which referentiality is subordinated' (Shaw 1998, pp. 49, 50). The real value of the idea of a Post-Boom, then, is not merely to describe the new, more referentially oriented writing that has emerged after the Boom, but to illustrate and explain the very interaction with the Boom which led to a dynamic of change that began in and around 1970.

Social referentiality and the Post-Boom

Having said all of the above, the idea of some kind of mainstream Post-Boom based on social referentiality is given an appearance of solidity by other developments between the 1970s and the 1990s. Two such developments are the emergence of – as they are called – *testimonio* and the New Historical Novel, both of which reinforce the impression of a greater emphasis on the direct presentation of social reality.

Testimonio or testimonial writing is a kind of autobiography told by another (usually more educated and narratorially gifted) person. The Mexican Elena Poniatowska (1933–) did much to make *testimonio* fashionable in certain circles, but the most famous example of the genre is *Me llamo Rigoberta Menchú y así me nació la conciencia* (tr. 'I Rigoberta Menchú, an Indian Woman in Guatemala', 1983). A harrowing account of the brutal treatment of a Guatemalan Indian community, the book gained eyewitness and campaigner Rigoberta Menchú the Nobel Peace Prize in 1992. A few years later, though, the North American anthropologist David Stoll's explosive exposé of alleged falsehoods and inconsistencies in Rigoberta's testimony, *Rigoberta Menchú and the Story of all Poor Guatemalans* (1998), brought into the open many debates about the authenticity of *testimonio*. Rigoberta's account was, of course, like other *testimonios*, edited and presented by someone else (in this case, Venezuelan anthropologist Elisabeth Burgos-Debray). Thus, while *testimonio* gives voice to the ordinary or marginalized people, it risks setting up the same tensions between presentation and reality that characterized the earlier fiction it seemed to be a reaction against.[13]

The New Historical Novel, posited by critic Seymour Menton in 1993, represented another obvious attempt to recuperate reality (albeit here in a more literary way), particularly by revisiting certain protagonists of the colonial and Independence periods. Abel Posse's (1936–) *Los perros del paraíso* ('The Dogs of Paradise'), from Argentina in 1983, is a much cited example. But Posse was born as far back as 1936 and other practitioners of the genre are Carpentier, Fuentes and Vargas Llosa, who are equally linked to the Boom (and before). And Augusto Roa Bastos' massively difficult 1974 fictional 'autobiography' of nineteenth-century Paraguayan absolute dictator Dr José Gaspar Rodríguez de Francia, *Yo el Supremo* (see chapter 4), in deconstructing historical discourse and generating a dynamic and open language, problematizes the very relationship between history and reality. In linking history to the unreliability of fiction, the New Historical Novel's worthwhile revisionism also harks back to a central idea of the New Novel of the Boom. As in *testimonio*, the connection to referentiality is strong, but still fundamentally problematic.

Of course, a very real problem is the intervention of academic or other 'intellectual' discourse in the production of these generic terms. The temporal projection of the Post-Boom corresponds with a period of consolidation of the reputation of Latin American literature in Northern and Western universities and in the international literary establishment and market. Though it is true to say that Cuban intellectual Roberto Fernández Retamar's *Calibán* functioned as a manifesto which promoted the production and dissemination of testimonial novels, the idea of *testimonio* as an object of critical examination gained prominence in the 1980s and 1990s thanks to its being embraced by the North American and then European academies (see chapter 7). The New Historical Novel is equally a critical category, as is the even more arbitrary 'novel of exile', which is also sometimes associated with the Post-Boom (see Shaw 1998, e.g. p. 79). *Testimonio*, for example, had been around for some time,[14] something which prompts the question of whether its subsequent canonization by the academy in the later twentieth century provided fuel for those critics wishing to perceive a more socially and reality-oriented Post-Boom.

The 1970s onwards also saw the politicization of academic discourse in literary studies in North American and UK universities (see chapter 7). In this consciously ideologically charged atmosphere, it became tempting to see the drive towards political reality perceived in the Post-Boom as a response to the rise of terror, authoritarianism and military dictatorship in Central America and the Southern Cone. Thus writers like Argentina's Luisa Valenzuela (1938–) or Ricardo Piglia (1941–) and Chile's Diamela Eltit (1949–) came to be included in some accounts of the Post-Boom, even though their tortuous and sometimes barely penetrable style, if in many ways politically challenging, has little to do with a transparent brand of referentiality. Indeed entry to the international market (be that the literary market or the peculiar economy of the modern university) in some sense depended on a critical muddying of the waters between political referentiality and experimental play. At a time of a relative crisis of legitimacy in the humanities, the former was necessary to render the discipline 'useful' or 'relevant', while the latter helped to preserve the traditional guarantees of academic intellectual respectability.

Thus the reliability of terms like the Post-Boom is a real problem. There is no doubt that the terrible political events of the 1970s and 1980s did foment political fiction, but the (often highly theorized and intellectualized) fiction so produced did not always necessarily fit the referential model *à la* Skármeta outlined earlier. Nor is it clear that these events were a material factor in the creation of the Post-Boom, which seems to have already been under way by the time of, say, the military dictatorships in Argentina and Chile, and seems in any case to have literary as much as political roots. It once again appears that the term 'Post-Boom' is most useful to mark a moment or period of reaction and renewal in relation to the Boom itself, rather than to cover comprehensively the thirty or so years of literary production that have followed it.

Women writers and the Post-Boom: Isabel Allende

One good illustration of the sorts of problem just discussed is the tendency to include the category of 'women writers' (or, sometimes, 'gay and lesbian writers') in the category of the Post-Boom, as if the emergence of such groups as literary phenomena were in some sense dependent on a literary rather than material shift in circumstances. In part, the choice to study such groupings is as much a manifestation of the history of universities and other institutions as it is one of literary history (see chapter 7). Indeed our awareness of certain female, gay or lesbian (or, of course, straight male) authors may have much to do with their promotion via the academy or its values and interests.

The discomfort of some academic critics with the success of Isabel Allende (1942–) (relative to the valorization of a writer like her – for many – more politically and intellectually acceptable fellow Chilean Eltit) is an interesting case. Allende is routinely included amongst lists of women of the Post-Boom, often in the company of writers with whom she has little in common. This has led to some ambiguities in her classification: in a 1997 encyclopedia of Latin American literature (long awaited by professional Hispanists), she did not receive a proper entry of her own, but was merely included in an entry for 'Best-Sellers' (Smith 1997). This was bizarre, since she is clearly, in terms of her international success and impact, a much more important figure than someone like, say, Skármeta. This is an indication of the aforementioned awkwardness in some critics about recognizing the genuinely popular and accessible dimension of Post-Boom writing, and hints at a lingering hankering after the intellectual complexity or even elitism of the Boom.

The fact is that Allende is one of the best representatives of both main views of the Post-Boom discussed here: she embodies both, on the one hand, a relationship to and reorientation of the novel of the Boom, and, on the other, the trend towards readability, structural clarity, socio-political commentary and relative optimism. Her *La casa de los espíritus* ('The House of the Spirits', 1982), a key work of the Post-Boom, is an unmistakable reflection of modern Latin American history and, in particular, the modern history of Chile up to the awful aftermath of the Pinochet coup. But in directly reflecting that history, the novel also functions as a commentary on the evasive nature of the narrative of the Boom, in particular García Márquez's *Cien años de soledad*.

It is arguable that the consistent use of fantasy and ambiguity in the Colombian's novel actually undermines its political effectiveness, and, while Allende has been criticized for mimicking *Cien años*, her novel is really a critical reworking of it. One character comments that 'no era partidaria de repetir los nombres en la familia, porque eso siembra confusión en los cuadernos de anotar' ('she did not approve of the repetition of family names across the generations, because that would sew confusion in her notebooks')[15] – a thinly disguised poke at the potentially perplexing repetition of names in the García Márquez book.

Moreover, the character's name is Clara (connoting clarity) and her notebooks, though not chronological, are not wilfully obscure like the manuscripts of García Márquez's Melquíades that they echo, and are (again unlike Melquíades' parchments) easily put in to order by a family member of a subsequent generation so that the facts are saved from the nebulous world of fantasy (p. 219). Indeed the entire structure of the novel could be seen to overturn its own early pattern of fantasy and replace it with a kind of harsh realism following the harrowing political realities of the coup: the spirits largely disappear and the novel builds up to a chapter entitled 'La hora de la verdad' ('The Moment of Truth'). As was suggested earlier, García Márquez's seminal text may be a rather equivocal model for the Boom, but, none the less, Allende's novel perfectly demonstrates the idea of the Post-Boom as a rearticulation of the Boom, while also exhibiting the trend towards greater referentiality that some associate with a Post-Boom proper.

Recent directions: McOndo and Crack

Inevitably, all terms beginning with 'Post-' are potentially problematic. In a sense, what has been suggested here is a spectrum of possible ways of understanding the Latin American Post-Boom, ranging across: a moment of rupture with a perceived Boom aesthetic; a rejection of a Boom aesthetic; a new relationship with a Boom aesthetic, which is now retuned and revitalized; a tendency away from the textual ambiguity of the Boom and towards greater social referentiality, characterized perhaps by a transitional period leading eventually to a mainstream Post-Boom typified by a more straightforward engagement with reality; or a long-running continuum covering a gamut of approaches from documentalism to non-referentiality. The problem with the last position is that it effectively reduces (or extends) the Post-Boom to refer to almost anything that has been published in Spanish America after the Boom. As a concept, then, its use is limited. Given the inevitable variety of types of fiction since the Boom, perhaps the term is most productively employed to refer to a type of fiction that is constituted by a sense of rupture with the Boom while remaining in some way connected to or in interaction with the Boom novel's underlying ideas. The point is that, even if the Boom was a finite material phenomenon, the idea of it has still, at the beginning of the twenty-first century, not been supplanted by a Post-Boom proper.

It would be instructive to consider, for example, the recent phenomena of McOndo and the Crack generation. In 1996 the Chileans Alberto Fuguet (1964–) and Sergio Gómez (1962–) published a collection of works by Spanish American writers born after 1960. Entitled *McOndo*, the book – with its pun on the name of García Márquez's fantastical invention of the town of Macondo – is clearly a reaction against the weight of Magical Realism, a denomination which gained international prominence thanks to the success of the Boom, and something Fuguet has described as 'a sort of curse that has afflicted novelists, filmmakers and tour guides all over the Americas'.[16] There is still, in other words, a sense that 'young' Latin American writers feel overshadowed by the Boom and feel a need to respond to it or challenge it. In the specific case of the McOndo writers, the perception that the new Latin America is a world of McDonald's, Mac computers and condos provokes a trend away from the exploration of national identities towards a new 'pop' conception of the local, saturated by North American influence and the processes of globalization – what Fuguet in another pun (on the name of the cross-borders NAFTA agreement) calls FTAA – a new Free Trade Area of the Americas sensibility. This seems essentially a refinement of a certain Post-Boom ethos of the 1970s and 1980s updated to a contemporary context.

An illustrative example of such an ethos is Peruvian Jaime Bayly's (1965–) *La noche es virgen* ('Virgin is the Night'). Bayly was a contributor to the *McOndo* book and his aforementioned novel won Spain's Herralde Prize after its publication in 1997. The novel is essentially a pop-cultural version of the stock Peruvian theme of *Lima la horrible* ('Lima the horrible').[17] The capital is presented as a sweaty, stinking, teeming cesspool, but mainly via the world of rock venues, sleazy clubs, drugs, booze and illicit sex. The main character is Gabriel Barrios, a middle-class gay/bisexual and cocaine addict, and much of the novel charts the fun- and frustration-filled excesses of his sexual and narcotic adventures. However, the power of the text really comes from Gabriel's frenetically paced first-person narrative, which captures wonderfully not only his own camp sensibility but also the feel of the cocky urban slang of the streets and clubs of Lima at the end of the twentieth century. But the exuberance of the drug-fuelled discourse is not necessarily matched by the content, which is ultimately rather dark. Gabriel's drug habit is in many ways an embarrassing form of escape: it marks him as apart from the bourgeois world from which he emanates (indicated in his run-ins with his own conservative mother and the mother of his would-be lover Mariano), yet is also a way of avoiding facing up to or coming to balanced terms with his identity. His sexuality remains, in essence, closeted and his self-expression therefore limited, as he does not want to risk any threat to his comfortable upper-class lifestyle as a TV show host and son of a well-to-do family. Indeed his sense of alienation is expressed via a rather self-damaging snobbery towards lower social and racial classes, including 'los brownies' ('non-whites'), as he colourfully but pejoratively refers to them. Though he valorizes Miami, to where he frequently repairs on shopping trips, there is a sense that pop-culture consumerism leaves him dissatisfied and tied to a Lima that is ultimately third world and dismal.

The novel ends with him alone at night on the capital's dingy streets, swallowing bitter cocaine tears and concluding that: 'no puedo seguir siendo gay y coquero en lima. me estoy matando. lima me está matando' ('i can't carry on being gay and a cokehead in lima. i'm killing myself. lima is killing me').[18] For all that the extravagance, youthful energy and aggressive contemporariness of Bayly's narrative promise a counter-Boom project, the traditional theme of Lima's apparent vibrancy actually being a stultifying microcosm of chaos and limitation links the novel to the past and, in some ways, does not progress us much beyond a 1969 Boom novel like Vargas Llosa's *Conversación en La Catedral*, which has, in the end, a remarkably similar tone.

The link between this born-after-1960 generation and the Boom is underlined by Fuentes' characterization (in yet another pun) of such new writers as eventually forming part of a 'Boomerang' generation. The self-styled Mexican 'generación del Crack', associated principally with writers Jorge Volpi (1968–) and Ignacio Padilla (1968–), uses for its sobriquet a pun that echoes the term 'Boom' while suggesting a break with it (and indeed they seem to favour a more 'intelligent' style of writing – which could be seen as a return to the Boom as much as anything). What has been most commented on about their most successful novels – respectively *En busca de Klingsor* ('In Search of Klingsor', 1999) and *Amphitryon* (tr. 'Shadow without a Name',

2000) – is their setting, in part, in the non-American environment of Nazi Europe and their basis in European intellectualism. This may suggest a break, but Europeanism was precisely a criticism of the novel of the Boom.

Unsurprisingly, in one interview Volpi is identified with a desire for differentiation from 'la etiqueta Boom' ('the Boom label'), while citing some of his principal influences as 'Carlos Fuentes, Vargas Llosa, los escritores del "Boom", Borges, etc.'.[19] A reading of a novel like *En busca de Klingsor* (winner of the 1999 Biblioteca Breve Prize) would give the impression that what Volpi is actually reacting against is a perceived 'light' strain in the later New Narrative that has come to be associated with a Post-Boom. This superb work is worthy of comparison with novels by successful middle-to-high-brow professional writers from Britain, other European countries and North America, like, say, Michael Frayn, Stephen L. Carter or even Umberto Eco. The novel, which is both intellectually challenging and thrillingly suspenseful, is built around modern science, in particular relativity and quantum theory and the quest to build the atomic bomb. Taking us through the lives and theories of Einstein, Gödel, Heisenberg, Schrödinger and Bohr (among others), the story deals with the American physicist Francis Bacon's military mission in post-war Germany to identify a mysterious figure codenamed Klingsor, who was thought to be Hitler's leading advisor on the atomic bomb.

Apart from the Spanish language and a certain explanatory tendency in the exposition of European history, there is little to suggest a specifically Latin American perspective here. If anything, the tone is reminiscent of the alleged universalist scepticism of Borges. This is built into the plot itself, whose resolution remains enigmatic despite the superficial illusion of closure, and is carried into the many theoretical reflections that pepper the text. The role of science, for example, is investigated in a way that prompts questions on the nature of truth and the human tendency to construct artificial patterns of order. And, in a typically Borgesian twist, Klingsor himself, the unseen manipulator pulling the strings in the shadows, is surely identifiable with God, the manufacturing of belief, and the questionable impulse behind creativity and the quest for meaning: one character asks if Klingsor 'no era más que una abstracción de nuestras mentes, una proyección desorbitada de nuestra incertidumbre, un modo de colmar nuestro vacío' ('just some kind of mental abstraction of ours, a wild projection of our uncertainty, a way to fill our void'), while Bacon speculates that Klingsor may be no more than 'una manera de justificar su investigación, asumiendo riesgos inexistentes e inventándose su propia tarea' ('a means of justifying his investigation, in which he was assuming non-existent risks and inventing his own task as he went along').[20] There is also, in the wartime and post-war context, a counterbalancing discourse of history, free will and the morality of choice (echoes of Fuentes here, another Boom figure).

However, as with Borges, the ultimate sense is that ideas (in their myriad variants) are used not so much in their own right as philosophy but rather as primarily the material for the fabrication of a rich and teasingly satisfying literary experience. Though without the artificial structural pyrotechnics of some Boom novels, the serious yet playful, complex yet compelling quality of their eminently marketable professional fictions makes the likes of Volpi and Padilla, if anything, the true heirs of the Boom.

In conclusion, then, it seems that the notion of a Post-Boom proper must be treated with caution. The Post-Boom clearly does mark some kind of rupture, but, like postmodernism, it is above all a state of mind: a state of mind in which a sense of newness is conceived in terms of the past as well as the present and the future.[21]

CHAPTER 6

Hispanic American Fiction of the United States

The history of Latin American fiction has always been bound up with the world beyond its borders: with the idea of Europe and, increasingly, North America. As has been seen, the narrative of the subcontinent has wrestled continually with notions such as the colonial heritage, independence, progress along foreign models, economic dependency and neo-colonialism, the autochthonous versus the cosmopolitan, specificity versus universalism, a literary modernity associated with the foreign, globalization and mass culture. From the nineteenth century and especially in the twentieth century and beyond, consciousness of Latin America's position within a larger American continent has contributed to shaping the direction of thought and artistic production. A shared and changing border has for some time been a key element in the identity and culture of Mexico, in particular, and what came to be referred to as the North American Southwest. Exile in the United States of America has long been a factor in the output of Latin American writers and intellectuals. In the twentieth century, patterns of mass migration from Mexico and the Caribbean (and, more recently, from elsewhere, especially Central America) began a growing process of Hispanicization within the United States itself. 'Latin America' effectively burst its borders and began to flow into the North. As the twentieth century developed, huge new communities of people born in the USA of Latin American descent took root and evolved. Americans of Hispanic descent have become a massive social, political and economic presence, and by the mid-twenty-first century will be one of the largest and most influential social groupings in the country. The effect on cultural activity generally and literary production in particular has been and will continue to be remarkable.

Describing the Hispanic peoples of North America is a problem fraught with difficulties of definition and nomenclature. Are we speaking of Latin Americans living in (sometimes) temporary exile, new immigrants from Latin America, or individuals born in North America of Latin American descent? In terms of the literature they produce, are we speaking of writing in Spanish, English or some Spanglish fusion of the two? How unitary is the question of Latin American provenance or descent? Are not Mexican Americans, Puerto Ricans, Dominicans and Cubans widely differing entities? And are there not large differences within the components of these individual community groups? Are the very terms used to describe them – Hispanic or Latino – meaningful or pejorative?

There are no easy answers to these questions. However, for the purposes of this or any discussion, some classificatory choices have to be made. In terms of writing, Latin American exiles or migrants will be largely excluded. Post-Boom writers like Argentina's Luisa Valenzuela and Chile's Isabel Allende have lived or live in North America and write about the North American experience. Valenzuela's *Novela negra con argentinos* ('Black Novel with Argentines', 1990) is based on her own experience of temporary exile in New York City and deals with the exile experience of Argentine intellectuals in the city, in the aftermath of displacement following the military dictatorship's Dirty War, begun in the late 1970s. Allende moved to California in 1987 and married an American in 1988. Her *El Plan Infinito* ('The Infinite Plan', 1991) is set in America and has an American protagonist, who finds salvation living and working in a Latino *barrio* or neighbourhood. *Hija de la fortuna* ('Daughter of Fortune', 1998) is a historical romance concerning Chilean migration and the Californian Gold Rush of 1848 onwards. Yet Valenzuela and Allende are not really considered anything other than Latin American writers, writing for a wider Spanish-speaking audience and not specifically for a North American market (though translations of Allende novels are big business in the US and other non-Spanish-speaking countries).

This does not mean that there are not or have not been Latino writers writing in Spanish for a North American Hispanic audience. However, most notably from the 1970s onwards, Latino fiction written in English has emerged as the principal manifestation of Hispanic writing in the US, and this is what will receive emphasis here. The themes of this fiction are mainly to do with the Hispanic experience in the US, but, especially more recently, some novels have concentrated on the original homeland too. A notable example of this last kind of novel is Sandra Benítez's (1941–) powerful and moving *The Weight of all Things* (2000), which recreates a young Salvadorean boy's experience of the assassination of Archbishop Oscar Arnulfo Romero and a massacre of *campesinos* or country folk at the Sumpul River in 1980 (though of Puerto Rican descent, Benítez lived in El Salvador).

None the less, it is Hispanic fiction dealing, by and large, with the US experience that has produced the really big names of Latino writing, especially from the 1980s onwards: Oscar Hijuelos (1951–), Sandra Cisneros (1954–), Julia Alvarez (1950–), Cristina Garcia (1958–) and Ana Castillo (1953–). But are these writers Hispanic or Latino? In practice the terms are used loosely and interchangeably (and will be here), though a strict definition might suggest that Hispanics are those born in Latin America who come to reside in the USA, while Latinos are those who have been born or educated in the USA itself.[1] Yet even these terms elide a considerable degree of difference. Cisneros and Castillo are of Mexican descent, while Hijuelos is of Cuban descent, Alvarez comes from a Dominican Republic family, and Garcia was born in Cuba. Before considering a sample selection of some major novels of US Latinos, the varying cultural roots of the Hispanic American experience must first be briefly traced.

Mexican Americans

The longest tradition of Hispanic writing in the US belongs to the Chicano or Mexican American community. Given that much of the North American Southwest belonged to Mexico until 1848, or 1836 in the case of Texas, Chicano writing has a lengthy and mixed history. Though there was both colonial and Latin American literary output in the region, literature in English did not really appear until the late nineteenth and early twentieth centuries. And more change came in the twentieth century when Spanish-speaking writers like Mariano Azuela (see chapter 2) came to North America in the wake of the fallout of the Mexican Revolution. A Chicano consciousness as such, however, did not really begin to emerge until after 1943, the year of the so-called Zoot Suit Riots, in which US servicemen attacked Mexican Americans in Los Angeles. The unequal status of Chicanos now began to come to the fore of the Mexican American mind and a political sense of Chicano identity began to grow. It was not until the 1960s, though, that this sense of identity solidified and was thus able to produce a recognizably Chicano aesthetic in literature. Chicanos were mobilized by the Civil Rights movement and also organized by the famous farm workers' leader César Chávez (1927–93). A Chicano movement grew, focused on a sense of a shared cause (*La causa* as it was known). This was aided culturally by the plays of Luis Valdez (1940–), a self-proclaimed *campesino* theatre that staged short plays for farm workers explicitly showing their exploitation. The famous epic poem, often read out loud at public meetings, 'I am Joaquín' (1967) by Rodolfo 'Corky' Gonzales (1928–), added to this increasing mood of oppositional collective identity.

What began was known as the Chicano Renaissance (the *florecimiento chicano*). But it was not until the 1970s that Chicano narrative began to take off. Two spurs were important. The first was the rise of literary journals, the most famous of which were *Aztlán* and the *Revista Chicano-Riqueña*. The title of the latter brings out the sense of a Chicano and Puerto Rican cultural critical mass in the USA, while the title of the former alludes to a fundamental myth that helped shape a Chicano mentality and aesthetic – the idea of an originary sacred place that embodies the essential Chicano spirit, under threat from Mexican American absorption into capitalism. The second spur was the Quinto Sol Press, which promoted a self-consciously Chicano narrative via publications and the impact of its influential Quinto Sol Prize. Chicano narrative now developed steadily, with a cluster of novels in the 1970s about male immigration and growing up, and a remarkable flourishing of English-language fiction in the 1980s, particularly by women, which to some degree broke with the by now conservative male-oriented and myth-obsessed vision, and integrated Chicano writing into something close to the mainstream of US literary production.

So what were or are these Chicano fictions? Before critics started debates about dating, the first Chicano novel was generally thought to be *Pocho* (1959) by José Antonio Villarreal (1924–). The importance of the novel lies in its exploration of the tensions between

Mexican and American identity: it concerns the family of an exile from the Mexican Revolution in which the children are torn between traditional Mexican values and the new US culture in which they live. However, John Rechy's (1934–) *City of Night* (1963) had a more mixed reception because of its (autobiographical) treatment of homosexual themes and gay prostitution, underlining the inherent social conservatism of the new Chicano cultural scene. The four Quinto Sol Prize-winning books, though, helped cement the growing reputation of Chicano fiction: . . . *y no se lo tragó la tierra* (tr. '. . . and the Earth did not Devour Him', 1971) by Tomás Rivera (1935–84), *Bless Me, Ultima* (1972) by Rudolfo Anaya (1937–), *Klail City Death Trip* (1972) by Rolando Hinojosa-Smith (1929–), and *Rain of Scorpions* (1975) by Estela Portillo Trambley (1936–99). Equally important was the award of Cuba's prestigious Casa de las Américas Prize to Hinojosa-Smith in 1976 for his *Klail City y sus alrededores* ('Klail City and its Environs'), something which marked an international recognition of a distinctly Chicano literature. Indeed the 1970s saw the publication of a whole series of novels about Chicano life, covering both rural and urban settings.

However, it was in the 1980s that the main literary breakthrough came. This was when the two Chicago-raised women authors Sandra Cisneros and Ana Castillo made their reputations with works that combined a Chicano viewpoint with a more broadly accessible appeal. They were followed by other important women writers, such as Denise Chávez (1948–), Alma Villanueva (1944–) and Helena María Viramontes (1954–). This was also the decade when Chicano literature gained real international visibility, with the publication in 1989 of Richard Rodríguez's (1944–) memoir *Hunger of Memory*, a book which critiques Chicano separatism and promotes the idea of cultural integration. And, in a significant extension of the scope and intellectual sophistication of Chicano writing, two women produced hugely influential hybrid texts that problematized Chicano identity from a lesbian Chicana perspective. These were *Loving in the War Years* (1983) by Cherríe Moraga (1952–) and *Borderlands/La frontera* (1987) by Gloria Anzaldúa (1942–): canonized by the North American academy, these works are often seen as the high point of Chicana cultural output.[2] Some of these important Chicano works will be considered later along with representatives of the other Hispanic American traditions.

Puerto Rican Americans

The Puerto Rican American experience is rather different to the Mexican American one. Though there were writers and intellectuals in exile in North America in the nineteenth century, the Puerto Rican presence in the country is largely a function of twentieth-century US-influenced economic factors, and it is particularly associated with the urban environment, especially of New York City. Puerto Ricans began arriving, mainly to work in tobacco, as early as 1900 when the island of Puerto Rico became a US territory, with US citizenship available from 1917. But the serious migration started after Operation Bootstrap in the 1940s and 1950s. Designed to develop the island by offering incentives to US companies, it actually encouraged mass migration from the countryside by destabilizing the country's traditional agricultural economic base, and led to an influx of Puerto Ricans into New York, where many faced unemployment or badly paid and low-value jobs. The link with the US was reinforced by the granting of Free Associated State status to Puerto Rico in 1952.

There developed a tradition of Puerto Rican writing dealing with the events of these years and with the problems of immigrants in the US, though much of this was in Spanish and often written on the island itself. The best-known example of this kind of writing is probably Pedro Juan Soto's (1928–) *Spiks* (1954), reflecting his own experience of time spent living in the Bronx. However, following the trend of memoirs and articles about immigrant life, a number of gritty urban narratives began to be produced in English in the 1960s, and they often also sought specifically to capture the tone of New York Puerto Rican or Nuyorican language. The most famous was *Down these Mean Streets* (1967) by Piri Thomas (1928–), an Afro Puerto Rican American from Spanish Harlem, which painted a grim picture of life in the urban ghetto and prompted a number of semi-autobiographical works in a similar vein right through to the 1970s and beyond.

The most important literary developments, though, were actually in poetry rather than narrative, prompted by the Young Lords Party's championing of the cause of poor Puerto Rican immigrants in the 1960s. Poetry remains the main manifestation of Puerto Rican American literary writing. Nicholasa Mohr (1938–) did write some decent novels from the 1970s onwards, which were less dark and male-centred and were sometimes written from a child's perspective. The best Puerto Rican American novel, meantime, is probably *Line of the Sun* (1989), by the Georgia-based poet Judith Ortiz Cofer (1952–), which, in a vaguely Magical Realist style, tells the story of several generations through the eyes of a young woman. This style of semi-magical, female-oriented family saga became fairly typical of much Latina fiction in the US.[3]

Cuban and Dominican Americans

The case of Cuban Americans is different again, in that migration from Cuba was often politically as much as economically motivated. As with Puerto Rico, there is a long history of exiles in the US, dating back to the liberation movement. The most famous were the novelist and activist Cirilo Villaverde (1812–94) and the poet, *modernista* novelist and architect of much Latin American national and liberation discourse José Martí (1853–95). Other writers came to escape the regime of Fulgencio Batista from the 1930s to the 1950s, most notably Edmundo Desnoes (1930–). But the real waves of emigration began after the Cuban Revolution of 1959, with a marked rise in 1980 after the infamous Mariel Boatlift, when Fidel Castro ordered the exodus of over 12,000 Cubans to Florida in the USA in reaction to what was perceived as President Jimmy Carter's permissive attitude to Cuban political refugees. Among the Cuban writers who came to the US were Lino Novás Calvo (1905–83), Lydia Cabrera (1900–91), Enrique Labrador Ruiz (1902–90) and, most famously, Reinaldo Arenas (1943–90), whose novel *El portero* ('The Doorman', 1989) deals with a Cuban exile in Manhattan (Arenas committed suicide after contracting HIV and has become something of a cult figure).

Cuban American writing in English has become more prominent since the 1970s, though the focus is often different to that of Puerto Rican Americans, given the often middle-class provenance of Cuban exile. Two major novelists emerged in the late 1980s and 1990s. Oscar Hijuelos won the Pulitzer Prize for his 1989 novel *The Mambo Kings Play Songs of Love*, which became as much part of mainstream North American literature as anything else and has probably given Latino writing in the US a greater international projection than any other work. The other main novelist is Cristina García, whose national family sagas *Dreaming in Cuban* (1992) and *The Agüero Sisters* (1997) have had significant impact and travelled well.

A comparable Dominican American figure is Julia Alvarez. Her *How the Garcia Girls Lost their Accents* (1991) and *In the Time of the Butterflies* (1994) move between Dominican childhood and adult life in the USA. As with most Dominican writers, her work is marked by the dictatorship of Rafael Trujillo (1930–61) and the US intervention in the Dominican Republic of 1965. Dominican immigration in the USA did not become significant until the 1970s and 1980s. Most literary output is in the form of poetry and, though there are a number of short story writers and novelists, Alvarez is the one major, internationally recognized writer of fiction to have emerged.

One other female author who should be mentioned is Rosario Ferré (1942–), a Puerto Rican who is usually thought of as a Latin American writer, sometimes associated with the Post-Boom. However, her Puerto Rican saga *The House on the Lagoon* (1995) was an English-language novel and something of a hit in the USA and abroad. A well-known and largely Spanish-language author writing a major novel in English for primarily, one assumes, a US market is an interesting development in the history of Hispanic American fiction in the USA.

Some Writers of the 1980s and 1990s

Oscar Hijuelos

Though Hispanic fiction in the US has an identifiable history, it was really in the 1980s and 1990s that it transcended its ghetto or activist roots and came to prominence within the North American literary mainstream. This eighties and nineties Latino novel does display some features inherited from the modern Latin American tradition, most notably the post-García Márquez penchant for family sagas, but has never really reached the heights of its Spanish-language Latin American counterpart. Still, it represents a significant strand in US writing, has some international projection and has produced figures of note. Some notable examples from those mentioned above will now be sketched to complete this brief survey.

As has been said, *The Mambo Kings Play Songs of Love* (1989) marked the Latino novel's departure from the margins and became an international success for Oscar Hijuelos. He had already set the tone with *Our House in the Last World* (1983), which dealt with the experiences of a Cuban immigrant family in the 1940s, but without an emphasis on politics and struggle. *The Mambo Kings* is another tale of immigrant life whose main strength is really the evocation of time and place. It is about two brothers, Cesar and Nestor Castillo, who leave Havana in 1949 to come to New York City, where they set up a mambo and cha-cha band. The climax to their career is an appearance with Desi Arnaz on a highly popular TV programme, the *I Love Lucy* show. But the book is a typical tale of fleeting success followed by decline. Nestor is obsessed by a lost love, in whose memory he writes twenty-two versions of the romantic bolero 'Beautiful Maria of My Soul', and slowly self-destructs. After his brother's death, Cesar's life sinks into a dismal pattern of womanizing, drinking and pathetic attempts at a comeback. There is no sense of insight gained in the story of Cesar and, if anything, the novel must be taken as a comment on the illusory nature of the American dream. Yet it does bring a period thrillingly to life and manages to inject some optimism via the narrative perspective, which is that of Cesar's son, whose recreation of their lives gives them a certain dignity and immortality. An interesting anecdote is that the novel also achieved a degree of notoriety when Gloria Parker, leader of Glorious Gloria Parker and Her All-Girl Rumba Orchestra, launched a $15-million libel suit against Hijuelos, claiming her reputation had been ruined by the novel (the case was eventually dismissed).

But Hijuelos never really repeated the success of *The Mambo Kings*. His next two novels, *The Fourteen Sisters of Emilio Montez O'Brien* (1993) and *Empress of the Splendid Season* (1999), are notable, though, in that they shift the emphasis from machismo to female characters, illustrating the continuing development of Latino writing away from its early angry-young-man beginnings.

Sandra Cisneros and Ana Castillo

Indeed it was the appearance of a number of major female Latina novelists that really indicated a coming of age for the Hispanic novel in the US. Two Chicanas were particularly important in this take-off of Latin writing.

Sandra Cisneros' 1984 novel *The House on Mango Street* is something of a landmark. It certainly deals with issues of poverty, low self-esteem and degradation in the *barrio*, but via a gentle and unaggressive, female, poetic voice. The story is told in a series of poem-like vignettes from the perspective of an adolescent girl, Esperanza, who longs to have a room of her own in a fine house but retains a sense of connection to the crumbling little house on Mango Street where she grew up. This is a classic Chicano/a tale of cultural tensions between Latino/a roots and the American dream, then, but what is new is the lyrical, feminized and ultimately optimistic point of view. Cisneros' reputation grew with her collection of poems-cum-stories dealing in part with female sexuality and Latin background, *My Wicked, Wicked Ways* (1987), and her short story collection *Woman Hollering Creek* (1991). She is set, at the beginning of the twenty-first century, for international stardom with her massive, radiant, multigenerational novel about a Mexican American family, *Caramelo* (2002), which is the most significant large-scale contribution to Chicano literature so far and which also taps into an increasingly popular Latin American tradition of female-oriented, semi-historical family romances, started by Latin American writers like Isabel Allende and Laura Esquivel (Mexico, 1950–).

The other major Chicana writer to emerge in the 1980s was Ana Castillo. A feminist and activist in the 1970s, her two novels *The Mixiquiahuala Letters* (1986) and *Sapogonia* (1990) established her firmly as a force in Chicano narrative. The first is an epistolary novel based on letters sent by a Chicana woman to an American friend, which recount a series of sometimes real, sometimes imaginary travels and adventures involving a search for identity and roots. If a journey to Mexico helps the protagonist, Teresa, put her US Chicana identity back into perspective, *Sapogonia* still dwells on the idea of a mythical lost paradise of Mexican origin, though with perhaps a more romantic and less overtly political emphasis than that of earlier writers. These are relatively challenging works focused very much on issues of identity. Castillo's 1993 novel, *So Far From God*, is probably her most significant work for a wider audience. Accessible and entertaining, it paints a magical-real picture of a Chicana family in a small southwestern town, in what is one of the most vivid accounts of Chicano culture to date. Unfortunately, her 1999 work, *Peel My Love Like an Onion*, slips back into a less focused style, but none the less presents a lively account of a part-crippled flamenco dancer's Chicago-based sense of an identity that is both Mexican and American.

Cristina Garcia and Julia Alvarez

Unsurprisingly, given the longer and more politicized history of Chicano writing, the two women writers who joined Hijuelos in breaking down the barriers between ethnically Latino and broader North American fiction were Caribbean Americans: Cuban American Cristina Garcia and Dominican American Julia Alvarez. Their major novels appeared in the 1990s.

Garcia's early novel of a family divided by the Cuban Revolution, *Dreaming in Cuban* (1992), was followed in 1997 by a best-selling though technically sophisticated novel on a similar theme, *The Agüero Sisters*. The sisters of the title are Reina and Constancia, whose mutual estrangement is a reflection of the political scene. Reina lives in Cuba and supports the Revolution. Constancia is in the United States. Despite their different situations, though, both sisters have a similarly problematic relationship to the past. Constancia becomes obsessed by the unexplained death of her mother, Blanca, who, it transpires, betrayed her husband Ignacio sexually and was later shot by him (the father later committed suicide). The dark-skinned Reina, meantime, is the offspring of Blanca's affair with a mulatto and becomes wrapped up in the attempted reconstruction of her own past. Though indirectly, the convoluted family saga raises questions about nation, ethnicity and identity, as the sisters struggle to come to terms with and understand their cultural inheritance as it relates to their contemporary circumstances. But there is also a degree of reflection on what it means to be a Hispanic woman. Fidelity and punishment for transgression are matched here by images of strong and defiant women who challenge machista or masculine norms. Garcia's latest novel, *Monkey Hunting* (2003), is another multigenerational story, but this time about a less noted area, that of Chinese immigration into Cuba and the Chinese contribution to Cuban culture.

Like Garcia's earlier novels, Julia Alvarez's *How the Garcia Girls Lost their Accents* (1991) is also about sisters, but this time it is the familiar and entertaining story of how immigrant girls learn to reconcile their parents' traditional island values with the exciting new experiences being opened up to them in the USA of the 1960s onwards. Since this breakthrough novel, Alvarez's best works have been historical fictions. *In the Time of the Butterflies* (1994) is about the brutal murder of the Mirabal sisters – the founders of an underground movement against the Trujillo dictatorship in the Dominican Republic, called *Las Mariposas* or The Butterflies – in 1960, just after Alvarez's own family had been forced to flee the country. *In the Name of Salomé* (2000) concerns a humble mulatta who became a national poet in the Dominican Republic, Salomé Ureña (1850–97), and the retracing of her daughter's relationship to her from the USA. Once again, it offers a more revisionary, female-centred take on Latin identity.

Rosario Ferré

As Latino writing began firmly to enter the middle-brow mainstream, an interesting related phenomenon could be noted. Alongside the success of popular novels by Latin Americans in English translation, some Latin American, as opposed to – in a strict sense – US Latino, writers began to write novels in English. For example, the successful Havana-based Cuban author of noir crime novels, José Latour (1940–), has published the well-received *Outcast* (1999) and *Havana Best Friends* (2002). But the most famous and intriguing case, at least for critics, is probably that of Rosario Ferré, who published her *The House on the Lagoon* in 1995, followed later by *Eccentric Neighborhoods* (1998) and *Flight of the Swan* (2001). All of these novels are relatively accessible, but perhaps break with the overtly radical political and feminist agenda that Ferré appeared to espouse in the past when writing in Spanish.

The most famous, *The House on the Lagoon*, is on the surface a feminist, if derivative, rewriting of Puerto Rican history. Yet another family saga with light magical undertones posing as national history, it tells the story of the Mendizábal family, who represent the changing face of the island oligarchy against the background of the conflictive history of the island's relationship to the United States. The narrator Isabel, a supporter of Puerto Rican independence, eventually breaks free from her pro-North American husband Quintín, in a fairly obvious if, in the end, rather dramatic allegory of gender and political independence. But the principal technical feature of the novel – as with so many Boom and Post-Boom novels from Latin America – risks undermining the power of the allegory. Quintín finds and glosses his wife's narrative with his own version, with the effect that we are repeatedly reminded of the subjective and ambiguous nature of reality and the text's own status as self-conscious fiction. In the end, the novel seems something of a Latin confection to the recipe of a successful formula that will go down well with the English-language market. Or, more positively and from a more radical perspective, perhaps this is an example of the colonized playing the colonizers at their own game, by using the North American market for a Latin American writer's own ends.

Gloria Anzaldúa

The academic community's favourite Latina radical is without doubt the Chicana Gloria Alzandúa. She is really quite unlike the mainstream writers discussed here and does not even write fiction as such. Instead she produces a difficult, hybrid mixture of history, autobiography, poetry and fiction, which gives expression to her notion of the border as identity rather than just a literal barrier. Her *Borderlands/La frontera* (1987) has become something of a seminal work in certain critical circles. Its subtitle, *The New Mestiza*, indicates not only a connection with the traditional political focus of the Chicano movement, but also the desire to adopt and modify the movement's thinking to create a different, more plural and more dynamic notion of identity. Hence Alzandúa's personal emphasis on her own identity as a Chicana lesbian of colour, which inevitably involves resistance to an all-encompassing, white, middle-class notion of lesbian identity. The border itself is seen as being everywhere where people or cultures or identities interact or simply exist. In a sense, she is trying, like many other feminists in the 1980s, to transcend patriarchal binary logic and create a new, non-binary space for expressing and understanding identity.

At the same time, though, Alzandúa does seem to wish to reinterpret Mexican myth and history from a specifically female perspective. She appropriates problematic tropes to do this: for example, the vagina is presented as a wound that bleeds, a scar like the border itself, and a sign of the brutal origins of Latino culture in the European and perhaps later North American rape of land and/or people. And a complex exploration of Aztec history and myth seeks not only to recuperate the contribution of women but to propose an alternative originary ideal based on the creator figure, Coatlicue, both male and female, the embodiment of the dissolution of binary opposition and a more meaningful model of identity. Whether this sort of thing is to the taste of those who enjoy reading the likes of Hijuelos, Cisneros, Alvarez or Ferré is a matter of opinion. However, what is interesting about Latino cultural production is the way it has managed both to retain an oppositional political discourse and equally to enter the literary mainstream. What is less clear is how well it has managed to do the two things at the same time. Indeed many of the big cultural debates about both Latin American and US Latino fiction around the end of the twentieth century were precisely about the 'ethical' roles of literature and criticism, as the next chapter will discuss. These are debates that always have been and always will be about positions and choices, and that will therefore probably always and in their very nature remain ultimately irresolvable.

CHAPTER 7

Culture Wars: Ways of Reading Latin American Fiction

Any literary history or account of a literary phenomenon will always only be a version of that history or phenomenon. Indeed, in some ways, the account may even constitute the construction of the phenomenon itself. At a simple level, the selection of representative authors and texts will always be a matter of choice, most likely a choice based on the perpetuation of certain pre-existing bodies of opinion about which authors and texts are important or significant. More problematically, such a process of selection may even create the impression of the predominance of certain movements or trends which may be no more than the manifestation of certain patterns of critical values or beliefs. For example, the idea that the New Narrative and the Boom represent the key development in the evolution of Latin American letters may be little more than a critical projection, a projection which ignores the vast range of other types of literary output that have not been canonized by the branch of criticism that foregrounds the New Narrative and the Boom.

A central feature of literary criticism since, roughly, the 1970s onwards, both in general and in the particular context of Latin America, has been an increasing awareness of the relativity or partial nature of literary-critical judgements. Readers will be familiar with broad debates about canonicity, in which the literary establishment's construction of historical traditions based on great works has been scrutinized and challenged. More concretely in the case of Latin America, concern has been expressed about the imposition of European patterns of literary history on an entirely different cultural context in a way that has promoted limited, questionable or even false literary histories.

The problem is that the alternative literary histories generated by such a process of contestation are likely to be no less selective (indeed may be even more so) than the model they reject. Moreover, the new models proposed can tend to favour particular ways of approaching literature that may be just as likely to foster reductive or skewed perspectives as they are to encourage liberating ones. The endgame of such cultural debates is often the assertion of a contextual complexity that results in a peculiar mixture of extreme relativism coupled with occasions of narrow self-interest. What follows is a brief attempt to flesh out some of the debates about how to read and understand Latin American fiction, while avoiding the denial of a mainstream of literary history which, if problematic, does none the less represent the reality of the existence of dominant literary trends.

Rethinking the Boom

Let us begin with the Boom. Implicit in the literary history offered here may be the idea of the Boom as a pivotal or culminating moment. Latin American literary history seems to be a process of tension between tradition and modernity in which a modernist (in the broad Anglo-American sense) ethos gradually asserts itself against a perceived notion of tradition, climaxing in the scepticism and complexity of the New Narrative and the Boom, and followed by a further trend which is both reaction against and continuation of the climactic moment. Yet the Boom itself could be regarded as a fabrication of the market. Spanish agents and publishers, prestigious literary prizes, the professional ambitions of certain authors and their backers, literary magazines, the sales potential of translations of an area seen as new, and the rise of Latin American studies in US and other universities all combine to create the impression of a phenomenon (see chapter 4). And this phenomenon comes to be associated in the mind of readers and critics with Latin American literature itself. Thus the emergence of Latin American literature as an international phenomenon is indelibly linked to a particular and inevitably narrow version of it. Latin American literature becomes about the Boom and all other literary products of the subcontinent are now defined in relation to it. For instance, regional novels come to be seen as interesting only in that they embody the kind of traditionalism against which the New

Novel is thought to be a reaction. And European and North American university courses on Latin American literature come to be dominated from around the 1970s by the New Novel, and perhaps a few limited earlier 'classics', thereby reinforcing a particular perception of literary history.

The perceived 'newness' of Latin American literature is a factor here. In the 1960s and 1970s, university courses (and the research and journals that university departments produced) were dominated by Peninsular Spanish literature – above all, perhaps, the study of the Spanish Golden Age. As late as the mid-to-late 1980s, the introduction of Spanish American literature as a compulsory element for first- and second-year undergraduate students of Spanish was a source of controversy in the department where I spent much of the early part of my career. Latin American literature as a discipline, then, became bound up with the idea of the new, and this seemed to underscore the centrality of the Boom in the Latin American literary canon. Of course, all this had changed dramatically by the start of the twenty-first century. In British universities it is often said that the Golden Age is in a state of crisis, and it is probably almost easier in some universities to do a course on Latin American photography than it is on *Don Quijote*. The question is whether this shift indicates the fallacy of the centrality of the New Narrative or the arbitrariness of the subsequent reaction against the traditional canon.

Politics and the Boom

The fact remains that the rise in international literary criticism on Latin American fiction from the 1960s onwards came to be dominated by work on the New Narrative. But critics eventually came to see the Boom as a locus of privilege or elitism. The problem with the Boom for many critics was that it essentially took place in Europe. Most of the major novelists of the Boom had lived in Europe and their work was often promoted by Spanish publishing houses or non-Latin American translations. This led to a critical perception that the coming of age of the Latin American novel was part of a process of that novel's Europeanization, of its 'catching up' with the sophistication of European (or North American) modernist narrative. Before long, a key and repeated criticism made against many literary critics (and indeed literary writers) was that of Eurocentrism – the reading of Latin American culture through a European lens, the classification of Latin American literature according to European categories, and the validation of that literature according to its adherence to European standards of technical and philosophical expertise. This led ultimately to a whole trend in literary criticism in which the contextual specificity of Latin America came to be seen as paramount. More generally it led to a debate based on a conflict between the political and the universal, which has marked criticism on Latin American fiction ever since.

Two important works on the modern novel illustrate this difference: Gerald Martin's *Journeys Through the Labyrinth* (1989) and Donald Shaw's *Nueva narrativa hispanoamericana* (first published in 1981) can be taken to exemplify the two points of view.[1] Essentially critics were divided between those who saw the New Narrative as mainly worthy of interpretation with regard to its socio-political significance, and those who saw it as representing the abandonment of committed writing in favour of the exploration of metaphysical unease and of the nature of the human condition. As the preceding chapters have shown, a bald distinction between two such positions would be crude, and the evolution of fiction in Latin America involves a complex amalgam of both positions. The rise of literary theory in the final few decades of the twentieth century made terms like 'universal' and 'the human condition' seem untenable, and political approaches of one sort or another came to dominate the academy by the end of the century. But to deny the existential dimension of modern Latin American narrative (whether one chooses to see it as misconceived or not) would be a preposterous denial of literary history, and an illustration of the dangers of assuming that because a perception is currently in vogue it is somehow closer to the truth.

Theory and Post-structuralism

Oddly enough, the first real challenge to supposedly conventional readings of Latin American fiction came, albeit via a somewhat convoluted route, from Europe itself. From the 1960s many French academics were in the thrall of structuralism, and this led eventually to the ubiquity of post-structuralism and the general rise of what came to be known as 'theory'.[2] One figure worth mentioning here is the Cuban novelist Severo Sarduy, who studied and worked in Paris with leading French intellectuals and gurus of theory, and began to integrate the concerns of literary theory into his own literary work. But the real journey – though this is something of an oversimplification – made by literary theory was to the United States academy and then back across the Atlantic to the UK and elsewhere. By the early 1980s it had a grip on literary criticism, especially so in the 'new' areas of emphasis such as Latin American literature.

Initially, the challenge to conventional criticism was tied up with the idea of self-referentiality. The early work of Sharon Magnarelli on Donoso is a good example, with its accent on the wastefully excessive use of language that simply reveals the absence of a centre, a core or a meaning.[3] However, the work of Magnarelli and others rapidly evolved in a more political post-structuralist direction. A crucially influential work was Roberto González Echevarría's *Myth and Archive* (first published in 1990), which seeks to show how Latin American narrative has tended to reflect various types of discourse about reality rather than reality itself, culminating in the self-reflexivity of the modern narrative of the twentieth century. González Echevarría, who became a key player in the professional world of literary criticism, tries a tricky balancing act here, combining the idea of literature's basis in other literary texts, rather than in external reality, with a historicizing project linked to some awareness of social critique.

What happened more generally in literary criticism was that the emphasis on the irreducibilty of meaning soon came to be linked with the idea of a challenge to the ways in which meaning and values are conventionally articulated in Western, bourgeois society. Theory was soon beginning to function in the service of politics (inevitably so, its practitioners would argue), and the effect on criticism of Latin American literature was to be radical. To this day, in fact, criticism on Latin American literature is often characterized by the complex tone of variations on an inheritance of political post-structuralism. A sampling of some of the suggested further reading at the end of this study will allow individual readers to decide whether or not this has enhanced our understanding of Latin American fiction, or created an indulgent critical culture of pedantry and obfuscation.

A problem is that the institutional rise of theory has also corresponded temporally with a crisis of legitimacy in the humanities in universities. One might reasonably wonder if the surge in literary criticism of an extreme complexity of language, often coupled with some sort of attempted socio-political commentary, is itself an anxious desire to make literary criticism appear 'advanced' and 'productive', in a way which actually risks making it part of the very late-capitalist structures it so often appears to seek to critique.

'Latin Americanist' Criticism

A feature of the politicization of literary criticism has been the urge to identify a specifically Latin American tradition of literary criticism that is counter to the supposedly European-driven model. This altern-ative tradition has always existed, but has also been systematically disinterred in recent decades.[4] Latin American intellectuals, like Rodó and Martí, established towards the end of the nineteenth century the idea of literature as a key component in the expression of a funda-mentally Latin American identity, and commentators have often noted the large number of Latin American statesmen and even presidents who have also been literary writers. Latin American critics like the Dominican Pedro Henríquez Ureña and Venezuelan Mariano Picón Salas, who both taught in the US in the 1940s, were at the forefront of developing the idea of a specifically Spanish American cultural tradition, which needed to be explained to the outside world. Figures like Brazil's Antônio Cândido, Argentina's Alejandro Losada and Uruguay's Angel Rama later theorized Latin American literature within a much more explicitly social, economic and political framework.

The big name here is undoubtedly that of Angel Rama, now almost synonymous with the revindication of a specifically Latin American model of literary criticism. His most famous works are *Transculturación narrativa en América Latina* (1982) and *La ciudad letrada* (1984), the latter translated as *The Lettered City*. Rama popularized the notion of transculturation, referring to the complex ways in which cultures are mutually transformed through contact (as opposed to the one-way process of acculturation). This allowed him to posit a positive model of Latin American literature that was a kind of fusion of local culture and the avant-garde. He also asserted the civil duty of the intellectual as being in opposition to the authoritarian demands of the state.

Leaping forward, from here can be traced a link to the contemporary fashion for cultural studies. Its rise as a phenomenon is overdetermined and has multiple roots. Rama can be used as a link of sorts, though, in that he is essentially arguing for a type of writing that operates outside the ambit of conventional intellectual elites and interacts with popular culture. North American critics later followed with what came to be known as subaltern studies, which asked questions about the incorporation of subaltern perspectives into literature and knowledge. North American presses also came to include postcolonial and post-modernist approaches, with debates usually raging – in both cases – around questions of hybridity and the appropriateness or applicability of non-Latin American models to Latin American experience. Such debates, however, involved a new group of Latin American critics or thinkers, such as Néstor García Canclini, Nelly Richard and Beatriz Sarlo,[5] who are seen to theorize the Latin American cultural experience from within – though the selective adoption and co-option of such figures by areas of the American and European academy raise questions about how representative they are of Latin American thought. And, of course, a key knock-on effect of the rise of cultural studies and the fascination with popular culture is the challenge to the significance of literature itself, often now seen as by its very nature a manifestation of elitism in the face of more popular forms of cultural expression.

But perhaps the most striking feature of the critical trends outlined above is their meta-critical quality. They often involve little literary criticism as such, but, in so far as they do deal with literature, tend to dwell instead on the relationship of literature to culture, institutions, theory and professional debates. These powerful trends in cultural criticism are clearly some way from the model of literary history followed by and large here, but have become a central and important part of the academic study of literature in its cultural context.[6]

History, women and sexuality

There are, however, a number of notable ways in which the broad thrust towards a more political and Latin Americanist criticism has had a very clear impact on the nature of literary history and the study of literature traditionally understood. One is that the move away from a relentless focus on the New Narrative has given new impetus to studies of fiction from the nineteenth and early twentieth centuries. A distinguished example is Doris Sommer's *Foundational Fictions*. Important for its uncovering of gendered underpinnings to national discourse in historical romances of the nineteenth and early twentieth centuries, it also put neglected canonical classics like *Amalia* and *María* back on the literary critical map (see chapter 1) and helped encourage a general trend of new investigation into nineteenth-century literature. Also significant was Carlos Alonso's updating of understandings of early twentieth-century fiction in *The Spanish American Regional Novel*. Recently too there has been a flurry of works on the Spanish American *modernista* novel (see chapters 2 and 3). Works of this earlier period – especially the nineteenth century – are now being rediscovered and re-examined in their own right and in terms of contemporary critical thinking on nationalism and modernity, and not just as fodder for studies of what the New Narrative was rejecting in Latin American tradition.[7]

This is not without its dangers, of course: recuperation of texts by modern critics should not lead us to assume automatically that certain texts, like, say, *Sab* or the *modernista* novel, were more influential than they probably were in practice (see chapters 1 and 3). A similar caution should perhaps be exercised with another practical example of canonical recuperation or revision. A major trend in contemporary criticism has been the discovery of writers allegedly traditionally excluded from the canon, such as women writers or gay writers.[8] There is, of course, absolutely no problem with examining fiction in terms of gender or sexuality, and developments in these areas have considerably enriched our appreciation of many texts. However, one has to be careful when ascribing traditional literary-historical significance to such texts. Thus, Reinaldo Arenas is sometimes considered alongside Manuel Puig as a key figure in the Post-Boom; but Puig's unquestionable place in the emergence of the Post-Boom has little necessarily to do with his sexuality, while Arenas has probably come to public attention precisely because of his sexuality and related political significance rather than because he was influential in the development of a Post-Boom as such (see chapter 5).

Similarly, the emergence of women writers is sometimes described as partly constitutive of the Post-Boom, but is it fair to see, say, Luisa Valenzuela, Rosario Ferré, Marta Traba (Argentina, 1930–83) or Diamela Eltit as of equal significance with Isabel Allende? Some of the first group may owe something of their status in the new canon to the importance they have been granted precisely as women writers by critics operating in North American or European universities, rather than because of a crucially influential role in the development of literary trends in Latin America (see chapter 5). None the less, feminist criticism and a focus on women's writing are an important aspect of the politicization of literary criticism on Latin American fiction, and have probably been one of the most useful and productive antidotes to traditional modes of reading literature from the region.[9]

Conclusion

What this brief postscript on approaches to Latin American fiction has, hopefully, shown is that no literary history can be regarded as innocent or neutral. All critics have their preconceptions or agendas, and there are genuine ethical questions to be considered when metropolitan critics fix their gaze on cultures associated with the periphery. Equally, though, in the haste to disassemble an allegedly Western-influenced canon, there is a danger that an alternative new canon of marginality will be created that has even less inherent value than the one it is supposed to replace. And at the same time, hugely influential authors like Borges and Vargas Llosa cannot be simply written out of literary history because their politics no longer fit the new orthodoxies of the academy. The Boom, after all, did take place, and books like this would not be being written if it were not for the international projection that the New Narrative achieved for Latin American fiction. The history of Latin American fiction is inevitably bound up with politics, but the centrality of some literary trends and figures rather than others (though this notion is unpalatable to many after the rise of theory) must have something to do, not just with the political construction of taste, but with the fact that there is something particularly interesting or exciting about certain writers that makes people want to read their works more than others.

There is, in the end, such a thing as a mainstream, whether one approves of it or not. And there is the possibility of producing coherent literary histories which remain none the less sensitive to other potential reconfigurations of them. The account offered here can never hope to be a definitive one, but it can claim to be a legitimate portrait of how Latin American fiction has grown into the internationally recognized phenomenon that it now unquestionably is.

Notes

CHAPTER 1   BEGINNINGS: NARRATIVE AND
THE CHALLENGE OF NEW NATIONS

1   The examination of Latin American fiction offered in this book will
follow a conceptual as well as historical pattern and will be selective in
the choice of representative texts. For a broad-ranging survey covering
literature in general from the colonial period to the present day, see, for
example, Hart (1999). A good detailed account of the development of
fiction specifically, from the nineteenth century onwards, is Shaw (2002).
For a consideration of Latin American literature in its broader social,
political, cultural and historical context, see Swanson (2003). Two encyclo-
pedias are recommended: González Echevarría and Pupo-Walker (1996)
and Smith (1997). The best synoptic history of Latin America which also
contextualizes literary production is Williamson (1992). A useful shorter
history of Latin America is Fowler (2002). Full references to authors and
books mentioned in the notes and main text in the preceding fashion are
included in the further reading section of this book. Other references will
be given in full in the notes. Translations of titles and quotations are
usually mine, though 'tr.' (meaning 'translated as') is used where a text
is commonly known in English by a title which is not close to the
original Spanish or Portuguese.

2   The process of Independence, that is the break with a Catholic European monarchy and the establishment of republican self-rule, was a
variable process from place to place. The process in Chile and Mexico,
for instance, was somewhat different to that described for Argentina
here. In Brazil, there was initially a transition to a constitutional monarchy followed by eventual movement to a reasonably representative
government.

3   A survey of the theme of Civilization and Barbarism, from which some
    of the comments here stem, can be found in Swanson (2003).

4   Of course, with regard to Europe, Sarmiento also rejected Spanish tradi-
    tionalism with its implied colonial heritage.

5   Esteban Echeverría, *La cautiva/El matadero* (Buenos Aires: Huemul, 1977),
    pp. 144, 148.

6   For some examples of new types of sophisticated re-readings of Sarmiento
    and Echeverría in the modern period, see Alonso (1998) and Altamirano
    and Sarlo (1997).

7   For an attempt to identify some earlier candidates for the first
    Spanish American novel, see, for instance, Cedomil Goic, 'La novela
    hispanoamericana colonial', in *Historia de la literatura hispanoamericana*,
    vol. I (Madrid: Cátedra, 1982), pp. 369–406.

8   A useful piece on *El periquillo sarniento* from the modern period is Antonio
    Benítez Rojo, 'José Joaquín Fernández de Lizardi and the emergence
    of the Spanish American novel as national project' in Sommer (1999),
    pp. 199–213. See also Nancy Vogeley, *Lizardi and the Birth of the Novel in
    Spanish America* (Gainesville: University Press of Florida, 2001).

9   The case of the gaucho will be considered in more detail in the second
    chapter with regard to Ricardo Güiraldes' *Don Segundo Sombra* (1926).

10 Sommer (1991) is recommended reading for a sophisticated take from a
    modern perspective on a number of the national romances considered here.

11 Catherine Davies has produced an excellent and very helpful critical
    edition of the novel: Gertrudis Gómez de Avellaneda, *Sab* (Manchester:
    Manchester University Press, 2001). References are to this edition.

12 *Criolla* is the feminine form of *criollo*.

13 Two other representative novels not discussed here, but which the reader
    may wish to examine, are the Romantic *Clemencia* (1869) by Ignacio
    Altamirano (Mexico, 1834–93) and the more obviously costumbrist *Cecilia
    Valdés o La Loma del Angel* ('Cecilia Valdés or Angel's Hill', 1882) by Cirilo
    Villaverde (Cuba, 1812–94).

14 Clorinda Matto de Turner, *Aves sin nido* (Mexico City: Oasis, 1981),
    pp. 51–2.

15 The term *indio* or Indian was originally used to describe the inhabitants
    of the New World due to the misapprehension that Columbus had reached
    the Indies via a western route. The word came to be used to refer to the
    descendants of these people, though *indígena* is now often a more accept-
    able term, rendered in English via the adjective 'indigenous'.

16 Machado de Assis, *Dom Casmurro* (Rio de Janeiro: Edições de Ouro, nd.),
    pp. 265–6.

17 Helen Caldwell, *The Brazilian Othello of Machado de Assis: A Study of Dom
    Casmurro* (Berkeley, CA: University of California Press, 1960); John

Gledson, *The Deceptive Realism of Machado de Assis: A Dissenting Interpreta-tion of Dom Casmurro* (Liverpool: Francis Cairns, 1984).

CHAPTER 2   NATIONAL NARRATIVES: REGIONAL AND CONTINENTAL IDENTITIES

1 Pérez-Firmat (1982), p. 139.
2 Apart from those texts mentioned in n. 1 of chapter 1, a useful and detailed survey of twentieth-century Spanish American fiction, which incorporates a consideration of *modernismo* and the *vanguardia*, is Williams (2003). Williams gives details of a whole range of lesser-known novelists outside the scope of this study.
3 Ciro Alegría, *El mundo es ancho y ajeno* (Buenos Aires: Losada, 1977), p. 29.
4 Brazilian Regionalism will not be considered in detail in this chapter. Two key examples of drought novels are *A bagaçeira* ('Trash', 1928) by José Américo de Almeida (1887–1980) and *O quinze* ('Nineteen Fifteen', 1930) by Raquel de Queiroz (1910–2003). A more sophisticated, psycho-logical take on the novel of the *sertão* is the compelling *Vidas secas* ('Barren Lives', 1938) by Graciliano Ramos (1892–1953). An author who would become one of Brazil's most successful novelists as the twentieth century progressed, Jorge Amado (1912–2001), has written increasingly colourful regional novels centred mainly on the cocoa-producing area of Bahia. An important forerunner of Brazilian Regionalism and an influ-ential work throughout Latin America was *Os sertões* (tr. 'Rebellion in the Backlands', 1902) by Euclides da Cunha (1866–1909): a hybrid essay-cum-novel, the book brings the *sertão* to public consciousness and offers a pessimistic examination of the government's brutal suppression of a messianic peasant uprising at Canudos in 1896–7.
5 A sophisticated re-reading of Regionalism from a modern perspective is Alonso (1990).
6 Other notable examples of the genre are Martín Luis Guzmán (1887–1976), *El águila y la serpiente* ('The Eagle and the Serpent', 1928) and Nellie Campobello (1900–86), *Cartucho* (tr. 'Cartucho and My Mother's Hands', 1931). The novel of the Mexican Revolution can also be seen to extend well into the modern period with writers like Agustín Yáñez (1904–80), Juan Rulfo and Carlos Fuentes (see chapters 3 and 4).
7 Mariano Azuela, *Los de abajo* (London: Harrap, 1973), p. 123. A useful critical guide on the novel is Clive Griffin, *Azuela: Los de abajo* (London: Grant and Cutler, 1993). A helpful companion book is Rutherford (1971).
8 Positivism, based on the philosophy of Auguste Comte (1798–1857), became popular amongst the post-Independence elites (especially in Brazil)

because of its emphasis on the advancement of society through science and progress.

9   Rómulo Gallegos, *Doña Bárbara* (Madrid: Austral, 1982), p. 25.
10   A still useful critical guide on the novel is D. L. Shaw, *Gallegos: Doña Bárbara* (London: Grant and Cutler, 1971).
11   Ricardo Güiraldes, *Don Segundo Sombra* (Buenos Aires: Losada, 1939), p. 17.
12   A perceptive reading of this episode is Peter Beardsell, '*Don Segundo Sombra* and *Machismo*', *Forum for Modern Language Studies*, 17 (1981), 302–11. Beardsell also has a useful critical edition of the novel (Oxford: Pergamon, 1973).
13   See, for example, José Eustasio Rivera, *La vorágine* (Managua: Nueva Nicaragua, 1983), pp. 114–18. A useful critical guide to the novel is John Walker, *Rivera: La vorágine* (London: Grant and Cutler, 1988).
14   Horacio Quiroga, *Cuentos escogidos*, ed. Jean Franco (Oxford: Pergamon, 1973), p. 64. This is a useful introductory edition, with a representative selection of nature stories. A good flavour of Quiroga's work can be gained from the critical guide by Peter Beardsell, *Quiroga: Cuentos de amor de locura y de muerte* (London: Grant and Cutler, 1986). For a sophisticated reading from a modern perspective, see Alonso (1998).

CHAPTER 3   THE RISE OF THE NEW NARRATIVE

1   For discussions of the New Narrative, see, for example: Lindstrom (1994); Martin (1989); Shaw (1995, 2002); Swanson (1990), on which some comments here build; Williams (2003).
2   The best general account of *modernismo* is Jrade (1998).
3   For useful general accounts of *modernista* fiction, see Lindstrom (1994), Shaw (2002) and Williams (2003). For more detail, see González (1987) and Phillipps-López (1996).
4   For useful accounts of vanguard fiction, see Williams (2003) for an introduction and Pérez-Firmat (1982) for more detail.
5   Cuban essayist Roberto Fernández Retamar would later famously invert Rodó's opposition in, for example, his *Algunos usos de civilización y barbarie* (Buenos Aires: Contrapunto, 1976).
6   Rubén Darío, *Poesía* (Barcelona: Planeta, 1987), p. 147. Other *modernista* writers of fiction include, for instance: José Martí (Cuba, 1853–95), José Asunción Silva (Colombia, 1865–96), Luis Gonzaga Urbina (Mexico, 1868–1934), Amado Nervo (Mexico, 1870–1919) and Rafael Arévalo Martínez (Guatemala, 1884–1975).
7   Other figures who could be considered include, for example: Martín Adán (Peru, 1908–85), Jaime Torres Bodet (Mexico, 1902–74), Enrique

Labrador Ruiz (Cuba, 1902–91), Norah Lange (Argentina, 1906–72), Eduardo Mallea (Argentina, 1903–82) and Teresa de la Parra (Venezuela, 1889–1936).

8 Macedonio Fernández, *Papeles de Recienvenido. Continuación de la nada* (Buenos Aires: Losada, 1944), p. 128, and 'Doctrina estética de la novela', *Revista de las Indias*, July (1940), p. 417.

9 Quoted in Franco (1973), p. 219.

10 Roberto Arlt, *El juguete rabioso* (Buenos Aires: Losada, 1973), p. 96.

11 Arlt's key later novels are, for critics, his principal works, even though *El juguete rabioso* is probably better known and more historically significant. They are *Los siete locos* ('The Seven Madmen', 1929) and *Los lanzallamas* ('The Flamethrowers', 1931). Useful and accessible on Arlt is Paul Jordan, *Robert Arlt: A Narrative Journey* (London: King's College London Hispanic Series, 2000).

12 Ernesto Sábato, *El túnel* (Barcelona: Seix Barral, 1983), p. 134. Though now quite old, a decent introduction to Sábato is Harley D. Oberhelman, *Ernesto Sábato* (Boston: Twayne, 1970).

13 The best book on Onetti is probably Mark Millington, *Reading Onetti* (Liverpool: Francis Cairns, 1985). Also interesting, for the connections it establishes between Onetti and other authors, is Gustavo San Román (ed.), *Onetti and Others* (Albany, NY: State University of New York Press, 1999).

14 Jorge Luis Borges, *Ficciones* (Madrid: Alianza, 1979), p. 92.

15 Borges' other principal influential collection was *El aleph* ('The Aleph', 1949). Of the numerous works on Borges, it is difficult to suggest just one or two. Perhaps a starting point would be Harold Bloom (ed.), *Jorge Luis Borges* (New York: Chelsea House, 1986). There is also a still useful critical guide to *Ficciones*: D. L. Shaw, *Borges: Ficciones* (London: Grant and Cutler, 1976). The definitive biography is Edwin Williamson, *Borges: A Life* (New York and London: Viking, 2004).

16 See, for example, chapter 4 of Swanson (2003) or chapter 8 of Davies (2002).

17 The most obvious example is Beatriz Sarlo. See her *Jorge Luis Borges: A Writer on the Edge* (London: Verso, 1993).

18 Magical Realism is a multifaceted and much debated term. The best guide is Parkinson Zamora and Faris (1995). Planned at the time of writing is Hart and Ouyang (2005).

19 On Carpentier, see, for example, Roberto González Echevarría, *Alejo Carpentier: The Pilgrim at Home* (Austin, TX: Texas University Press, 1990).

20 Arguedas, like Onetti, Borges, Carpentier and others, continued to write into the Boom and will be mentioned again in that context in chapter 4. A still excellent book on Arguedas, which brings out well the stylistic

technique and offers a strong analysis of the rebellions mentioned, is William Rowe, *Mito e ideología en la obra de José María Arguedas* (Lima: Instituto Nacional de Cultura, 1979).

21 W. H. Gass, 'The First Seven Pages of the Boom', *Latin American Literary Review*, 29 (1987), 33–56.

22 Miguel Angel Asturias, *El Señor Presidente* (Buenos Aires: Losada, 1948), p. 215.

23 The *esperpento*, referring to grotesque people or things, was a term used by the Spaniard Ramón del Valle Inclán (1866–1936) to describe a dramatic and narrative technique of systematic distortion.

24 A useful analysis of the novel is the essay by Gerald Martin in Swanson (1990), pp. 50–73.

25 This is Shaw's view. See, for example, Shaw (2002), pp. 125–6. For a fuller analysis of the novel, see the essay by Peter Beardsell in Swanson (1990), pp. 74–95.

26 Juan Rulfo, *Pedro Páramo* (Mexico City: Fondo de Cultura Económica, 1977), pp. 7, 12.

CHAPTER 4   THE BOOM

1 For an excellent account of the Spanish American novel in Spain, see Santana (2000).

2 See n. 1, chapter 3.

3 Decisions here about the inclusion of figures associated with the Boom are necessarily taken on a selective basis. Amongst other names which could be considered are: Jorge Amado (see chapter 3), Antônio Callado (Brazil, 1917–97), Autran Dourado (Brazil, 1926–), Jorge Edwards (Chile, 1931–), Salvador Garmendia (Venezuela, 1928–2001), Elena Garro (Mexico, 1920–98), Adriano González León (Venezuela, 1931–), José Lezama Lima (Cuba, 1910–76) and David Viñas (Argentina, 1929–).

4 The best introduction to Cortázar is Peter Standish, *Understanding Julio Cortázar* (Columbia, SC: University of South Carolina Press, 2001). For a challenging reading of Cortázar from a more theoretically inflected perspective, see Carlos J. Alonso (ed.), *Julio Cortázar: New Readings* (Cambridge: Cambridge University Press, 1998).

5 Julio Cortázar, *Rayuela* (Barcelona: Edhasa, 1979), p. 15.

6 Julio Cortázar, *Todos los fuegos el fuego* (Barcelona: Edhasa, 1977), p. 101.

7 An excellent book built around the tension between nationalism and cosmopolitanism in relation to modernity in Fuentes is Maarten van Delden, *Carlos Fuentes, Mexico, and Modernity* (Nashville: Vanderbilt University Press, 1998). Also recommended is Steven Boldy, *The Narrative*

of Carlos Fuentes: Family, Text, Nation (Durham: University of Durham, 2002).

8 See Carlos Fuentes, *La muerte de Artemio Cruz* (Mexico City: Fondo de cultura económica, 1978), p. 129.

9 See, for example, n. 9, chapter 3.

10 An excellent account of the creative process in Vargas Llosa is Efraín Kristal, *The Temptation of the Word: The Novels of Mario Vargas Llosa* (Nashville: Vanderbilt University Press, 1998). One of the best introductions to Vargas Llosa is Sara Castro-Klarén, *Understanding Mario Vargas Llosa* (Columbia, SC: University of South Carolina Press, 1990).

11 One of the criticisms made against Vargas Llosa is the apparent shift in his treatment of natives, the interior and the Civilization-versus-Barbarism conflict in his work from, roughly, the mid-1970s onwards, though this change – whether one approves or not – seems broadly in line with his own political development.

12 García Márquez has written many other novels, but the canonical New Novel of the 1960s, *Cien años de soledad*, will be concentrated on here. In a way, his follow-up novel, *El otoño del patriarca*, is more typical of the New Narrative in that it employs a complex stylistic and structural pattern which the 1967 novel lacks. The critical literature on García Márquez is vast. Three recommendations are: Michael Bell, *Gabriel García Márquez* (London: Macmillan, 1993); Robin Fiddian (ed.), *García Márquez* (Harlow: Longman, 1995); and Bernard McGuirk and Richard Cardwell (eds.), *Gabriel García Márquez: New Readings* (Cambridge: Cambridge University Press, 1987).

13 Gabriel García Márquez, *Cien años de soledad* (Buenos Aires: Sudamericana, 1978), p. 21.

14 Augusto Roa Bastos, *Hijo de hombre* (Buenos Aires: Losada, 1976), p. 274. A starting point on Roa Bastos is David William Foster, *Augusto Roa Bastos* (Boston: Twayne, 1978).

15 Donoso (1983) is a valuable insider's account of the history of the Latin American Boom. On Donoso, see Philip Swanson, *José Donoso: The Boom and Beyond* (Liverpool: Francis Cairns, 1988), and Sharon Magnarelli, *Understanding José Donoso* (Columbia, SC: University of South Carolina Press, 1993).

16 José Donoso, *El obsceno pájaro de la noche* (Barcelona: Seix Barral, 1979), p. 237.

CHAPTER 5   AFTER THE BOOM

1 Pamela Bacarisse, 'Manuel Puig: *Boquitas pintadas*', in Swanson (1990), p. 207. A useful introduction by Bacarisse is *The Necessary Dream: The*

Novels of Manuel Puig (Cardiff: University of Wales Press, 1988). There is an excellent biography of Puig: Suzanne Jill Levine, *Manuel Puig and the Spider Woman* (Madison, WI: University of Wisconsin Press, 2001). For references to criticism on writers already established in the Boom, see chapter 4. Useful books on the Post-Boom, apart from the general works on Latin American fiction mentioned in earlier chapters, are Swanson (1995), Williams (1997) and, above all, Shaw (1998).

2   The emphasis here will be on fiction from Spanish America. However, there are parallel developments in Brazil, in particular with regard to a certain crisis of faith in modernism provoked by military dictatorship and the ensuing economic crisis in the 1980s. Brazilian fiction after 1970 remains heterogeneous, but there can be identified trends such as the re-emergence of a realist aesthetic, the growth of a perceived postmodern scepticism, and the rise of women writers. Two notable figures who could be considered as related to the Post-Boom are Rubem Fonseca (1925–), whose novels sometimes exploit the detective genre, and Silviano Santiago (1936–), best known for his boundary-breaking, gay-themed and New York-based novel *Stella Manhattan* (1985).

3   José Promis Ojeda, 'La desintegración del orden en la novela de José Donoso', in Antonio Cornejo Polar (ed.), *José Donoso. La destrucción de un mundo* (Buenos Aires: Fernando García Cambeiro, 1975), p. 203.

4   Interview with Z. Nelly Martínez, *Hispamérica*, 21 (1978), p. 53.

5   José Donoso, 'Dos mundos americanos', *El Mercurio (Artes y Letras)* (14 November 1982), p. 1.

6   José Donoso, *Casa de campo* (Barcelona: Seix Barral, 1980), p. 54.

7   See Shaw (1998) and Donald Shaw, *Antonio Skármeta and the Post Boom* (Hanover: Ediciones del Norte, 1994).

8   See chapter 1 of Shaw (1998). Skármeta's essays are referred to on p. 7 and provide a complementary perspective to the comments already discussed of a practitioner such as Donoso, who was formerly associated with the Boom.

9   Ronald Schwartz, *Nomads, Exiles and Emigrés. The Rebirth of the Latin American Narrative, 1960–80* (Metuchen, NJ, and London: Scarecrow Press, 1980), p. 99.

10   Interview with Emir Rodríguez Monegal, *Mundo Nuevo*, 2 (1966), p. 25.

11   See, for example, Severo Sarduy, 'El barroco y el neobarrocco', in César Fernando Moreno (ed.), *América latina en su literatura* (Mexico City: Siglo XXI, 1972), p. 182.

12   Severo Sarduy, *Cobra* (Buenos Aires: Sudamericana, 1972), p. 66; Roberto González Echevarría, 'Plain Song: Sarduy's *Cobra*', *Contemporary Literature*, 28, 4 (1987), 437–59.

13 For an excellent account of such a tension in Poniatowska's *Hasta no verte Jesús mío* (tr. 'Until We Meet Again', 1969), see Lucille Kerr, *Reclaiming the Author: Figures and Fictions from Spanish America* (Durham, NC, and London: Duke University Press, 1992). Two good works on *testimonio* are G. Gugelberger, *The Real Thing: Testimonial Discourses and Latin America* (Durham, NC, and London: Duke University Press, 1996), and Elzbieta Sklodowska, *Testimonio hispanoamericano: historia, teoría, poética* (New York: Peter Lang, 1991).

14 *Testimonio* was effectively in existence during the Boom of the 1960s, one key work being Miguel Barnet's (1940–) Cuban *Biografía de un cimarrón* (tr. 'Autobiography of a Runaway Slave', 1966).

15 Isabel Allende, *La casa de los espíritus* (Barcelona: Plaza y Janés, 1985), p. 233. A useful critical guide is Lloyd Davies, *Allende: La casa de los espíritus* (London: Grant and Cutler, 2000).

16 Alberto Fuguet, 'Magical Neoliberalism', *Foreign Policy* (July–August, 2001).

17 The phrase has its origins in Sebastián Salazar Bondy's 1964 work *Lima la horrible*, which presents Lima in terms of a society that has never escaped the negative legacy of its colonial past.

18 Jaime Bayly, *La noche es virgen* (Barcelona: Anagrama, 1997), p. 189.

19 Anna Solana and Mercedes Serna, 'Jorge Volpi: "La novela es una forma de explorar el mundo"', *Babab*, 4 (September 2000). It is important to stress, incidentally, that Volpi's novels are by no means all set in Europe.

20 Jorge Volpi, *En busca de Klingsor* (Barcelona: Seix Barral, 2002), pp. 336, 153.

21 Other selected novelists not mentioned here include: associated with the Post-Boom (though for differing reasons) – Argentina's Mempo Giardinelli (1947–) and Sylvia Molloy (1938–); Cuba's Reinaldo Arenas (1943–90); Mexico's Carmen Boullosa (1954–), Laura Esquivel (1950–), Angeles Mastretta (1949–) and Gustavo Sainz (1940–); Peru's Alfredo Bryce Echenique (1939–); Puerto Rico's Rosario Ferré (1942–) and Luis Rafael Sánchez (1936–); associated with the McOndo and Crack 'generations' – Bolivia's Edmundo Paz Soldán (1967–); Colombia's Santiago Gamboa (1965–); Mexico's Eloy Urroz (1967–). I would like to acknowledge Cambridge University Press for allowing me to use here a version of a chapter by me from *The Cambridge Companion to the Latin American Novel*, ed. Efraín Kristal.

CHAPTER 6   HISPANIC AMERICAN FICTION OF THE UNITED STATES

1 See William Luis in Swanson (2003), p. 122. Luis' essay there (pp. 122–53) is a useful introduction, as are the essays by him, Luis Leal and

Manuel M. Martín-Rodríguez in González Echevarría and Pupo-Walker (1996), vol. 2, pp. 526–56 and 557–86. See also Luis (1997) and Zimmerman (1992). There are a number of useful essays in Lavonne and Ward (1990). The survey in this chapter is selective rather than comprehensive, and aims to introduce readers more familiar with specifically Latin American fiction to US Latino fiction. A good starting point for finding more Latino writers is Lauro Flores (ed.), *The Floating Borderlands: Twenty-five Years of US Hispanic Literature* (Seattle and London: University of Washington Press, 1998).

2 Two useful surveys of Chicano literature are Tatum (1982) and Lattin (1986). For a more sophisticated, theoretically inflected reading, see Saldívar (1990).

3 The best book that deals with Puerto Rican literature in the USA is probably Flores (1991). Note, 'Latina' is the feminine form of 'Latino'.

CHAPTER 7   CULTURE WARS: WAYS OF READING LATIN AMERICAN FICTION

1 For a discussion of these two works, see chapter 1 of Swanson (1995). For a response by Martin, see his essay in Shaw (1995), pp. 117–31.

2 It is not the place of this book to explore issues in critical theory. A good early account is Catherine Belsey, *Critical Practice* (London: Methuen, 1980). For students new to theory, a helpful starting point is Peter Barry, *Beginning Theory* (Manchester and New York: Manchester University Press, 1995).

3 See the comments on Magnarelli in Swanson (1990), pp. 191–3 and 204, n. 17.

4 A good survey of this and wider trends in criticism is the essay by Brian Gollnick in Swanson (2003), pp. 107–21. Useful surveys on criticism within Spanish America and Brazil respectively are those by Aníbal González and K. David Jackson in González Echevarría and Pupo-Walker (1996), vol. 2, pp. 425–57, and vol. 3, pp. 329–44. A good book on political cultural criticism in Latin America is D'Allemand (2000).

5 More or less comparable figures from Brazil are, for instance, Haroldo de Campos, Roberto Schwarz and Silviano Santiago.

6 The discussion above is, of necessity, highly telescoped. The reader is referred to Hart and Young (2003) for a very useful introduction to cultural studies. A good sense of the tone of the debates referred to can be gleaned from Beverley, Oviedo and Aronna (1995). An excellent study of literature's relationship to popular culture in Latin America is Rowe and Schelling (1991). On postcolonial approaches, see Fiddian (2000). US Latino

fiction is also often seen in terms of debates about strategies for cultural identities and practices. See, for example, Poblete (2003).

7   See also Masiello (1992).
8   On the latter, see Foster (1991). For a theorized approach, see Quiroga (2000).
9   Good examples are Castillo (1992), Kaminsky (1993) and Brooksbank Jones and Davies (1996).

Further Reading

What follows is a list of references and a selection of suggested further reading, concentrating on works written in English. Guidance to most of these works is contained in the main text and notes. References to selected recommended reading on individual authors or specialized topics can be found in the notes.

Aching, G. 1997: *The Politics of Spanish American Modernismo*. Cambridge: Cambridge University Press.

Alonso, C. 1990: *The Spanish American Regional Novel*. Cambridge: Cambridge University Press.

Alonso, C. 1998: *The Burden of Modernity*. New York: Oxford University Press.

Altamirano, C. and B. Sarlo 1997: *Ensayos argentinos: De Sarmiento a la vanguardia*. Buenos Aires: Ariel.

Alvarez Borland, I. 1998: *Cuban-American Literature of Exile*. Charlottesville, VA: University Press of Virginia.

Armstrong, P. 1999: *Third World Literary Fortunes: Brazilian Literature and its International Reception*. Lewisburg: Bucknell University Press.

Barradas, E. 1998: *Partes de un todo: Ensayos y notas sobre literatura puertorriqueña en los Estados Unidos*. San Juan: Editorial de la Universidad de Puerto Rico.

Beardsell, P. 2000: *Europe and Latin America*. Manchester: Manchester University Press.

Beverley, J. 1999: *Subalternity and Representation*. Durham, NC: Duke University Press.

Beverley, J., J. Oviedo and M. Aronna (eds.) 1994: *The Postmodernism Debate in Latin America*. Durham, NC: Duke University Press.

Brooksbank Jones, A. and C. Davies 1996: *Latin American Women's Writing: Feminist Readings in Theory and Crisis*. New York: Clarendon Press.

Castillo, D. 1992: *Talking Back: Toward a Latin American Feminist Literary Criticism*. Ithaca, NY, and London: Cornell University Press.

Christian, K. 1997: *Show and Tell: Identity as Performance in US Latino/a Fiction*. Albuquerque: University of New Mexico Press.

Colás, S. 1994: *Postmodernity in Latin America: The Argentine Paradigm*. Durham, NC: Duke University Press.

Coonrod Martínez, E. 2001: *Before the Boom: Latin American Revolutionary Novels of the 1920s*. Lanham and Oxford: University Press of America.

D'Allemand, P. 2000: *Latin American Cultural Criticism*. Lewiston, Queenston and Lampeter: Edwin Mellen.

Davies, C. (ed.) 2002: *The Companion to Hispanic Studies*. London: Arnold.

Donoso, J. 1983: *Historia personal del 'boom'*. Barcelona: Seix Barral.

Fiddian, R. (ed.) 2000: *Postcolonial Perspectives on the Cultures of Latin America and Lusophone Africa*. Liverpool: Liverpool University Press.

Flores, J. 1991: *Divided Borders*. Houston: Arte Público Press.

Foster, D. W. 1991: *Gay and Lesbian Themes in Latin American Writing*. Austin: University of Texas Press.

Fowler, W. 2002: *Latin America: 1800–2000*. London: Arnold.

Franco, J. 1973: *Spanish American Literature since Independence*. London: Ernest Benn.

Franco, J. 1999: *Critical Passions: Selected Essays*. Durham, NC: Duke University Press.

Fuentes, C. 1969: *La nueva novela hispanoamericana*. Mexico: Joaquín Mortiz.

González, A. 1987: *La novela modernista hispanoamericana*. Madrid: Gredos.

González Echevarría, R. 1985: *The Voice of the Masters*. Austin: University of Texas Press.

González Echevarría, R. 1998: *Myth and Archive*. Durham, NC: Duke University Press.

González Echevarría, R. and E. Pupo-Walker (eds.) 1996: *The Cambridge History of Latin American Literature*. 3 vols. Cambridge: Cambridge University Press.

Hart, S. 1999: *A Companion to Spanish-American Literature*. London: Tamesis.

Hart, S. and W. Ouyang (eds.) 2005. *A Companion to Magical Realism*. London: Tamesis.

Hart, S. and R. Young (eds.) 2003: *Contemporary Latin American Cultural Studies*. London: Arnold.

Horno-Delgado, A., E. Ortega, N. M. Scott and N. Saporta Sternbach 1989: *Breaking Boundaries: Latina Writing and Critical Readings*. Amherst: University of Massachusetts Press.

Jrade, C. L. 1998: *Modernismo, Modernity and the Development of Spanish American Literature*. Austin: University of Texas Press.

Kaminsky, A. 1993: *Reading the Body Politic: Feminist Criticism and Latin American Women Writers*. Minneapolis and London: University of Minnesota Press.

King, J. (ed.) 2004: *The Cambridge Companion to Modern Latin American Culture.* Cambridge: Cambridge University Press.

Lattin, V. (ed.) 1986: *Contemporary Chicano Fiction.* Binghampton: Bilingual Review Press.

Lavonne, R. and J. W. Ward Jr (eds.) 1990: *Redefining American Literary History.* New York: Modern Library Association.

Levinson, B. 2001: *The Ends of Literature: The Latin American 'Boom' and the Neoliberal Marketplace.* Stanford, CA: Stanford University Press.

Lindstrom, N. 1994: *Twentieth-century Latin American Fiction.* Austin: University of Texas Press.

Luis, W. 1984: *Voices from Under: Black Narrative in Latin America and the Caribbean.* Westport, CT: Greenwood Press.

Luis, W. 1997: *Dance Between Two Cultures: Latino Caribbean Literature Written in the United States.* Nashville: Vanderbilt University Press.

Magnarelli, S. 1985: *The Lost Rib: Female Characters in the Spanish-American Novel.* Lewisburg: Bucknell University Press.

Martin, G. 1989: *Journeys through the Labyrinth.* London: Verso.

Masiello, F. 1992: *Between Civilization and Barbarism.* Lincoln, NE: University of Nebraska Press.

McCracken, E. 1999: *New Latina Narrative: The Feminine Space of Postmodern Ethnicity.* Tucson, AZ: University of Arizona Press.

Menton, S. 1993: *Latin America's New Historical Novel.* Austin: University of Texas Press.

Parkinson Zamora, L. 1997: *The Usable Past: The Imagination of History in Recent Fiction of the Americas.* Cambridge: Cambridge University Press.

Parkinson Zamora, L. and W. B. Faris (eds.) 1995: *Magical Realism: Theory, History, Community.* Durham, NC: Duke University Press.

Pérez-Firmat, G. 1982: *Idle Fictions: The Hispanic Vanguard Novel, 1926–1934.* Durham, NC: Duke University Press.

Phillipps-López, D. 1996: *La novela hispanoamericana del modernismo.* Geneva: Slatkine.

Poblete, J. (ed.) 2003: *Critical Latin American and Latino Studies.* Minneapolis and London: University of Minnesota Press.

Quiroga, J. 2000: *Tropics of Desire.* New York: New York University Press.

Rama, A. 1996: *The Lettered City.* Durham, NC: Duke University Press.

Ramos, J. 2001: *Divergent Modernities.* Durham, NC: Duke University Press.

Rossman, C. (ed.) 1987: *After the Boom: Recent Latin American Fiction.* Special edition of *Contemporary Literature*, 28 (4).

Rowe, W. and V. Schelling 1991: *Memory and Modernity.* London: Verso.

Rutherford, J. D. 1971: *Mexican Society during the Revolution: A Literary Approach.* Oxford: Oxford University Press.

Saldívar, R. 1990: *Chicano Narrative: The Dialectics of Difference*. Madison: University of Wisconsin Press.

Santana, M. 2000: *Foreigners in the Homeland: The Spanish American New Novel in Spain, 1962–74*. Lewisburg: Bucknell University Press.

Shaw, D. L. (ed.) 1995: *The Post-Boom in Spanish American Fiction*. Special edition of *Studies in Twentieth Century Literature*, 19 (1).

Shaw, D. L. 1998: *The Post-Boom in Spanish American Fiction*. Albany, NY: State University of New York Press.

Shaw, D. L. 1999: *Nueva narrativa hispanoamericana*, 6th edn. Madrid: Cátedra.

Shaw, D. L. 2002: *A Companion to Modern Spanish American Fiction*. London: Tamesis.

Shaw, D. L. and H. Méndez-Ramírez (eds.) 2002: *Spanish American Fiction in the 1990s*. Special edition of *South Atlantic Review*, 67 (4).

Smith, V. (ed.) 1997: *Encyclopedia of Latin American Literature*. London and Chicago: Fitzroy Dearborn.

Sommer, D. 1991: *Foundational Fictions: The National Romances of Latin America*. Berkeley, CA: University of California Press.

Sommer, D. (ed.) 1999: *The Places of History: Regionalism Revisited in Latin America*. Durham, NC: Duke University Press.

Spitta, S. 1995: *Between Two Waters: Narratives of Transculturation in Latin America*. Houston: Rice University Press.

Swanson, P. (ed.) 1990: *Landmarks in Modern Latin American Fiction*. London: Routledge.

Swanson, P. 1995: *The New Novel in Latin America: Politics and Popular Culture after the Boom*. Manchester and New York: Manchester University Press.

Swanson, P. (ed.) 2003: *The Companion to Latin American Studies*. London: Arnold.

Tatum, C. 1982: *Chicano Literature*. Boston: Twayne.

Williams, R. L. 1997: *The Postmodern Novel in Latin America: Politics, Culture and the Crisis of Truth*. Basingstoke: Macmillan.

Williams, R. L. 2003: *The Twentieth-century Spanish American Novel*. Austin: University of Texas Press.

Williamson, E. 1992: *The Penguin History of Latin America*. London: Allen Lane.

Yúdice, G., J. Franco and J. Flores (eds.) 1992: *On Edge: The Crisis of Contemporary Latin American Culture*. Minneapolis and London: University of Minnesota Press.

Zavala, I. M. 1992: *Colonialism and Culture: Hispanic Modernism and the Social Imaginary*. Bloomington and Indianapolis: Indiana University Press.

Zimmerman, M. 1992: *US Latino Literature*. Chicago: March/Abrazo Press.

Index